HAROLD M. MALLETT has had plenty of practical experience in family counseling. Not only does he have a family of his own in which to practice what he preaches, but he also has an extensive background in counseling others. He is senior pastor of the First Presbyterian Church, Lawrence, Kansas.

Keeping Peace in the Family

Keeping Peace in the Family

Harold M. Mallett

Nashville   Abingdon Press   New York

KEEPING PEACE IN THE FAMILY

Copyright © 1973 by Abingdon Press

Library of Congress Cataloging in Publication Data

MALLETT, HAROLD M. Keeping peace in the family.
1. Family life education. 2. Marriage counseling—United
States. I. Title
HQ10.M367   362.8′2   72-14276

ISBN 0-687-20762-2

Scripture quotation noted NEB is from the New English Bible,
copyright © the Delegates of the Oxford University Press and
the Syndics of the Cambridge University Press, 1961, 1970.
Reprinted by permission.

Lines from "Common Sense" from *The Face Is Familiar* by
Ogden Nash, used by permission of Little, Brown and Co.
Copyright, 1931, by Ogden Nash.

MANUFACTURED BY THE PARTHENON PRESS AT
NASHVILLE, TENNESSEE, UNITED STATES OF AMERICA

No writer could pay all his debts to others. He only confesses he could not have produced his work alone.

My deep gratitude is offered to:

My wife, Jean, to whom this book is dedicated. Since our college days together, we have been students of what spells "good family";

The family of William and Iva Mallett, my parents—and my own children, Mark, Grant, Gordon, and Sara. They have demonstrated the principles of peace in the family.

Those who have opened family confidences to me. Their names are not used, and some details are disguised.

Preface

A process of fracturing has been operating in families since the Garden of Eden. Yet it becomes more tragic, some places and times. The United States in the last quarter of the twentieth century may set some kind of record.

You could probably discover a sample for each of the following within your nearest ten neighbors (some may have occurred at your own address) :

A family is seldom together—members off to so many non-home activities. Thus they separate day by day, vaguely aware of mutual joys, sharing, or needs.

Children spend most of each day away from their parents. Emotional alienation can easily follow physical absence. Baby-sitters can help fill voids, but there are inadequacies, and often disappointments, in "custodial" care. Here and there, very young children are left to themselves. A Kansas City counselor says that alcoholism in grade-school children is directly related to loneliness, as children begin nipping from wine bottles when parents are away.

Teen-agers pull out on the family. The generation gap

as the cause is oversimplification. A revolution in life-styles is a more appropriate description. Standards of morality, ethics, religion, and custom have been chopped at the roots by adolescents bent on doing their own (not the family's) thing.

Elderly folk have been sent to homes for geriatric care. Sometimes this is a practicable answer, either because of the needs of grandfather and grandmother, or because of the conditions at home. On the other hand, it is often a cruel blow. Any visitor to old people's homes can describe the lonely anguish of many residents. Good or bad, however, the point is that we have courted separation as the answer, and family unity thereby suffers another setback.

Finally, *divorces continue to increase.* Even the suggestions of term marriages (from one to ten years) build into the wedding vows the possibility, the likelihood, of husbands and wives not being able to work out life together over the long run.

Besides these family rifts, the news media report the variety of other examples:

Drug addiction

Homicides and suicides

Lawsuits over financial disagreements

Wills contested

Feuds

Mental and emotional illness

Cruelty, incest, persecution, felonies

George _____, both aggressor and victim in a shattered family, said, "Somebody ought to give a course on how to live with people you love. I've pulled so many unnecessary errors, I'm sure there has to be a better way. I've made F's all along. It would be great, simply great, to begin passing the course!"

Millions of others would agree.

George's comment sent me to my typewriter. Family peace is never automatic. It is created by concerned people who study the next step. Their methods are based on judgment and tact. They observe the laws of probabilities.

Motivation will begin the new day. The personnel manager for a large aircraft company has developed this measuring device:

A perfect score for
    talent,
        training, and
            motivation, is
10 x 10 x 10—or 1,000.

But if the prospective employee is zero in any of them, his total, of course, is zero. So motivation is a must,—the ignition of effort!

Say your family life has blisters. There should be a way to heal them. But no efforts can break through barriers of discouragement. Anyone who lacks incentive can only keep things bad or make them worse. Fractured families mend as their people *want them to.* Sometimes the best attempts will get you nowhere, but the one who cares, tries.

Most reasonable people should already know what to do to keep family peace. The record is, they don't.

If one family could be saved for every copy of this book printed, I would celebrate my efforts. The possibility itself is encouraging.

A new era for the family depends upon
how much people care,
how well they study the rules,
and how hard they try.

HAROLD M. MALLETT

Contents

1
Peace Is Something You Are

Anybody knows you don't make rabbit pie with a rabbit.

Yet, human nature strains to achieve goals, skipping the ingredients.

It can't be done.

". . . but first you catch your rabbit."

So caps the recipe for rabbit pie, which tradition labels "folk-Missouri." Here's what they call their "receipt":

"First you make your mixin's;
then you mix your makin's.
Next, you pop it into the oven until it's brown,
but not too brown—
But first you catch your rabbit!"

These pages are all about family peace—the skill of carving out a together life, with a minimum of hostility.

We'll deal with ideas and ideals,
techniques and tips,
principles and policies.

Peaceful instructions are as important as the recipe for rabbit pie. But the most important factor in family peace is *you*. What you do ranks in the uppers, but falls second to what you *are*.

Pleasure-and-pain govern us so we try to avoid facing ourselves. It wounds our egos to discover that we are a part of the problem.

If we can blame the lousy weather,
    a gnawing plantar wart
       or some clod at the office,
that takes off pressure. Guilt is labeled for the other person.

Ogden Nash put it,

> Why did the Lord give us agility,
> If not to escape responsibility?

Ellen Browne located the gentle culprit in her mirror. She had tried—in her way.

And the tensions around her weren't imaginary.

We'd have to begin with Ellen's father-in-law. Dad Browne was a widower, retired, but most of all, *nearby*. He was handy with tools and eager to help. Ellen called Dad to repair the toaster, watch the kids, pick up some thread.

Not so bad.

But Dad also appointed himself private tutor, a Mr. Ann Landers. He only wanted to help!

Help!

It all grated on Ellen—
    this constantly summing up "what was wrong with . . ."

    this giving the narrow-eye treatment to every situation.

Worst of all, he challenged her treatment of the girls.

"Do you think that was wise?"

Right there, in front of Teddi and Susan!

(Any grandpa will take lumps if he injects himself into his children's affairs. It's agony to know something important, but not be free to tell it!)

Ellen's strict rearing went to war with her natural feelings.

Honor your elders.

"Obey your parents in the Lord."

But translated to the Dad Browne presence, it meant *let him take over.*

So Ellen had perpetual emotional colic. Something was going to explode soon.

There was more.

Earl Browne was an all-American success—human, popular, one of the best contractors around. A citizen-avant, he accepted any committee offer, especially if it affected young people.

(Children need concerned adults, but Ellen resented Earl's neglect of his own.)

Placques of appreciation checkered the walls of his bustling office.

When Earl *had* a free evening, he usually went to the club, played cards, drank. Then he'd come home ready for a boozy sleep. Ugly words richocheted from bedroom to bathroom and back.

It was more than habitual sniping; a subtle game was being played. Ellen became the *Parent,* scolding her bad boy. Earl was the *Child.* Child often enjoyed irritating Parent. Parent was frantic about what to do with Child.

15

They hadn't had a family vacation for years. Soon the girls would be too old to enjoy traveling with their folks. Earl would pack off with friends to fish and hunt; Ellen had the girls and house and chores and bills and errands.

When she filed for divorce, her friends gasped: "What ever happened to the Brownes? They seemed like such ideal people!"

Ellen didn't really want the separation. She filed, as she put it, "to get Earl's attention."

Three months of evaluation brought them around. They are together again, cooperating in mending the old breaks.

The girls celebrate the new zing.

And Father Browne does chores without playing coach.

At this point, it is easy to say they are doing better than before. Directions from their counselors included the actions needed.

But beneath these overt agenda lay a personal challenge to Ellen and Earl. Expert therapy surfaced buried hostilities. Here they were treated on the *Adult* level.

The improved person was the basis for reconstruction.

Ellen admitted it: she had neatly kept a schedule that prevented her from facing herself.

She was a compulsive busybody. She had conjugated her attempts to get through in the verbs

to go,
to buy,
to take,
to try,
to do.

And if the agenda petered out, there was the escape corner—television.

So Ellen clutched the misconception that activism heals. She hoped there was always a repair that could be made. By being pragmatic, she was confident that crises would retreat.

But she had to "catch the rabbit."

Like a character in the cartoon "Pogo," she said, "We have spotted the enemy, and he is us!"

Ellen is not alone at the shrine of St. Vitus. The word to describe all Western activism is *epidemic*. We believe in movement. We live opposite the meditating people. We manipulate ourselves into the immediate.

Some nights we want to stay wide awake, so we sip coffee. It has caffeine, about three grains per cup. Other evenings, we need sleep, so we gulp a "downer." We overeat, then take reducing pharmaceuticals. Whatever it is— too much fat, too little weight; too much hair in unwelcome places, not enough on top—buy the remedy. Too tall? Clothes will correct that. Too short? Ditto. Too old, or young, too pale or dark; too mercurial or saturnine? Something will do the trick.

Carry this over into life together, and it becomes a deadly fib. We neglect one another at home, but make up for it by piling up Brownie points outside. This covers over what we aren't doing at the house. We hold back positive support, then try to buy our families off with apologies, a dinner, or a check. We delay being effectual with family needs, then plunge into something for the holy trinity—the town, the school, the church! We postpone gab sessions with our children and teen-agers, then

17

try to win them back across the generation gaps *we* have created.

So, then, we try to do *something*—anything—take a trip, buy a gift, see the psychologist, offer inducements, make deals or threats—whatever we hope will save the day again.

Ellen and Earl had to see it written big: they lived by the delusion that peace is a list of things to do.

Each one acted it out like this: "To heck with what I *am* to you; it's what I *try*. Then if the roof caves in, I get a new set of actions. I turn to fresh tactics."

The girls could fill in more details. They were provided with the latest and best.

They actually needed what money couldn't buy—their parents—not secondhand and tired, but something near the best of Dad and Mom. They were starved for unsophisticated love—the kind expressed person to person.

An aborigine mother, carrying her baby in a back-sling, actually outclasses the civilized "manager" here. Early contacts, body to body, transmit wordless messages of genuine concern.

There is something "gutsy" about it. Take this literally. A baby rabbit may not even stay alive unless it is licked by its mother. It's an unspoken ministry.

Obviously, humans don't lick their children like animals, but the parallel is keen. Early, this means caressing their bodies. Voice tone and soothing assurance tell children they're wanted.

Later comes daily concern—being present and interested. Falling in line are understanding and support, while teens reach for independence. Now parents foster nest-

stirring, until the twenty-one-year-old is in college, employment, marriage, or military service—on his own.

Ellen and Earl had things to do.

By the thousands.

But for Teddi and Susan, and themselves, *actions* followed *character*.

A TYPE OF BEING—this is the theme for the peace symphony.

As I look back over homes I've known, peace has been possible with this kind of person:

1. He tries to become real (meaning genuine, sincere).
2. He eliminates basic anxieties, hostilities, and prejudices.
3. He reaches for maturity, grows into an Adult.
4. He is humble enough to see his own faults.
5. He is unselfish.
6. He has faith in himself, others, and God.
7. He is available to those he loves.
8. He is a disciple of common sense.
9. He places human values first.
10. He is pleasant to live with.

Impossible to realize? *Perfectly?*

Of course!

When a Missourian wants rabbit pie, he really does! But first he catches the rabbit.

2
Having the Touch

Take Chapter One, and apply it to anything that excites
you—
    lowering your golf handicap,
      taking up chair-caning,
        learning to play bridge,
            or, in this case, helping to make your family
wonderful—the basic unit is still *you*.

Target number one: BE THE BEST YOU CAN, FOR WHAT-
EVER FOLLOWS.

But there is another goal, you in action: *how you
operate*.

☞ TACT ☜

Many well-meaning people need lessons on how to tran-
slate goodwill into practice.

Remember the littl girl's prayer—the one that gets to
you:

    *Dear God, make all bad people good,
    and all good people nice.*

That is the premium business of *tactics*.

20

Follow an action from your brain to the body. Here is the machinery of tact. It includes—

facial expressions,

body motion, gestures,

the uses of tongue and eyes and fingers—

what you decide to say and do—

in fact, ALL OF YOU.

Tact is from the Latin *tangere,* "to touch."

So your extemities express what you are, at center. From the mental to the manual—every transaction involves your personality equipment.

☞ CAUTION ☜

There is no perfect set of techniques. If there were, that could be disastrous, because you might become the Big Operator, who tries to swing deals. The goal of tactful family people is to develop—

manners	expressions	methods
conversation	thoughtfulness	conduct
tone	relationships	consideration

—to result in harmony.

Nothing is guaranteed to "work" every time. Your concern is to do the best thing as often as you can.

Some actions are more bound to succeed.

Their opposites have a record for losses, so we learn to score in the game of averages.

That means the dove of peace favors those who care about *probabilities.*

Let's say you want to improve your approaches. There are some blunders to avoid.

☞ HOW TO FLUNK THE COURSE ☜

1. *Be insensitive!*

Put this down where you *have* to see it: whatever you are must be related to the feelings of others!

The Spanish call it *sympatico*. Jesus put it clear and bright in the Golden Rule: DO AS YOU WOULD BE DONE BY. Forget that, and you will hurt and be hurt.

Examples are endless. You could consider people like birds, and see how they "befoul" the cage:

There is, of course, the parrot, who chatters of all hours, with little meaning.

Next comes the "me-me" fowl, who uses *I* and *me* constantly. This is only the beginning!

There's the broad-tailed sofa monopolizer,

the scissor-beaked interrupter,

the wondrous-warbler-of-how-great-things-used-to-be,

the ever-late preening peafowl,

the gossipy vulture, feeding on juicy reputations,

the eagle-eyed spy-bird that devours privacies,

and the road-runner, always headed for the door.

As you guessed, this home is for the birds!

Insensitivity heads the list, and is basic to all the rest of family failures.

2. *To get a "down slip" in family, always make decisions for others.*

The take-over is sometimes called for, though it's hard to find many good examples. If someone is sick, helpless, infantile, or senile, you might be the one who has to command control.

Otherwise, deciding what anyone else should do is a sure way to commit arson.

Marty G. shows the way to initiate trauma. On August 1, she announced to her family, "This Saturday (August 5) we will leave for vacation." Then she made a major campaign of convincing Tom and their teen-agers how well it would work out.

She had thought it through.

She made the arrangements.

She would see that everything came out all right!

But Tom had planned to roof the house. And the teenagers were looking forward to a visit from a friend who had moved away.

"Oh, I understand how it is," pursued Marty, "but let's try it *my* way—just blast off for a vacation, *all together!*"

The blast-off began a family earthquake.

Marty's fault: She tried to take over for the family—a benevolent but scheming dictator.

You could begin your list with this bad sample, then add many others, like

making financial decisions,

giving constant domestic suggestions,

choosing a vocation for someone else,

even picking friends, dates, husbands or wives!

3. *Make a habit of putting family people down.*
That is, if you want to intercept good feelings!

The ways in which this personal foul occurs are infinite.
Generally, they include inferences, insinuations, suspi-
cions;
they are leveled at veracity, sincerity, intelligence;
they are meant to belittle, denigrate, discourage;
and they're done by those who are hostile, sometimes cruel.

The sneaky part about putting family people down is
that we aren't always aware of it, and don't mean to.

If the one we wound is sweet and docile, we may never
learn how we have hurt.

If he is mercurial, quick to flash back, you now have
two people trying to wound each other. Every statement
is tipped with a mustard barb.

*Have you ever noticed, when you have "scored" by
embarrassing someone, how soon your victory shrinks?*

So—even though you may enjoy instant *touché*—draw
horns and a tail on every demon idea you have of trying
to cut somebody down.

4. *Be impatient.*

You can express this anti-love many ways. It's conveyed
in the tone of voice, your look, the things you say, the
way you act.

You interrupt. This is a keen insult. It means, "Whatever you're trying to say is unimportant, uninteresting, or
unnecessary. Listen to me. I couldn't care less what's on
your mind."

You fidget. It's done by many methods:
shifting from one foot to the other,

finger-tapping,
    clicking a ball-point pen from "write" to "off,"
    looking past the one speaking,
        foot-shuffling,
            knee-crossing and uncrossing,
                clearing the throat,
                    etc., etc., etc.!

5. *Impute motives to others.*

"Oh, I know what you're up to," says this bungler.
"You say it is for reasons A, B, or C, but you really did it for X, Y, or Z."

So he lays a land mine of suspicion. He doubts your honesty; he openly challenges your integrity. And if someone else hears it, the cut is deeper.

Highlight this: THE ONE WHO IMPUTES MOTIVES MAKES HIMSELF THE JUDGE. YOU ARE PUT ON DEFENSE.

I had finished a "conventional" sermon, probably rated G.

But it was an election year.

After the Benediction, a red-faced member speared me in the narthex:

"Well! There's no question about your choice for President!"

I quickly rummaged over what I had said. "What brought out that response?" He had taken an obscure sentence out of context, and made it mean what *he* thought!

He not only injured me by imputing motives to me.
He wrong-guessed my politics!

25

6. *Slight others in speech.*

This is sometimes unintentional; we accidentally offend. Hostilities frequently surface in unguarded words—the Freudian slip. Face value, the hurt is not always evident. Yet there is a kind of *jab*.

Examples:

A. *"I wouldn't know."*

You've asked a sensible question. You believed this person would be able to answer it. Of course, "I wouldn't know" *means* "I don't know." But the reply has a barb. It implies you're stupid for coming to him. "Why ask me! I'm not the one who would be able to answer. Go to someone who knows."

Better: "I am sorry, but I don't know."

B. *"While you've been talking, I've been thinking . . ."*

Well, that's not nice! While you have been talking, he could have been *listening*.

Better: "You have a good idea. It set me to thinking . . ."

C. *"This is interesting."*

Watch for that hidden chigger! The other party tells about something. What he says is "that" to you—meaning it belongs to him—his subject, his ideas.

But when you respond with *"This is interesting,"* you take it over, and make the topic yours—so your *reaction* becomes more important than his statement.

Picky-picky?

Not so small! It is conversational piracy to capture every conversation on your terms.

Better: "That is interesting" (then ask a question to prove it!) .

D. *"I don't care what you say . . ."*

That's your ugly credo about the discussion. You affront your talking partner. Nothing he says will affect you, so a polite dialogue has been killed.

Better: "I see your point. Maybe it could also be this way . . ."

There are many direct attacks that are rude. They are of course ruled out automatically, because insults are the weapons of warfare, not the tools of peace.

In ordinary exchange of sentences, honor other people. It is the method of the thoroughbred family person.

7. *Be careless with inter-people arrangements, to destroy peace.*

A Sunday afternoon wedding was scheduled for Bill and Bev.

Bill's dad, three brothers, and two sisters planned to go.

One brother, Bob, had his car in repair, and needed a ride. But he didn't tell the others, and they didn't check. Several of the family said later they thought Bob would be in "the other car."

Communication was zero, and nobody meant it to happen.

Ben backed his car out. "I wonder if Bob has a ride."

His wife replied, "Oh, I guess Dad will take him."

At the church, Dad asked, "Didn't you bring Bob?"

"No, didn't you?"

They all were sorry, and felt stupid. Bob would always remember he missed Bill's wedding.

The victim of such a SNAFU shouldn't explode when he's been abused. But, on the other hand, it didn't need to happen.

Peaceful people are also careful people.

8. *Air your family's dirty linen.*

This is done, you guessed it, by those who talk too much. They run on and on about private family affairs, because they prefer it to other material.

Often the account favors the one talking. So he has the fun of getting the story told his way.

Passing family weaknesses around is tasteless and tragic.

The family reputation is smudged, then exhibited. Its standing will never be the same. Many neighbors are natural scavengers. They tend to identify others by their peculiarities:

Henry Henricks—you know—the one who has the withered ear.

The Gullivants—oh, that's the family whose boy got high on drugs and held up Sam's Barbecue.

When these trials hit people, it's bad enough already; but to talk about it compounds the tragedy. And if it pertains to your own household, you perpetuate bad copy.

So don't be careless about your kin. Most family storms can be weathered if the crew is loyal.

IF YOU CAN'T SAY SOMETHING GOOD, DON'T TALK. Stop the spread of bad news.

Most of all, you will wish you could take it back some day.

Check back over your conversations.

Did you ever regret having NOT said something? Seldom!
Ever regret HAVING said something?

THE ACID TEST. If you tell something about your folks,
and feel good, you've protected them. If you feel bad about
what you've said, read it clear: YOU HAVE EXPOSED CLAS-
SIFIED INFORMATION!

Whatever may ail your family is nobody's business.

That is, not until YOU make it so.

ASSIGNMENT: Try to think about your tact as LOVING
MANNERS. This is thinking of others before you act.

If you grasp the idea of "one person, responsible for
himself," that's one up and the rest to go. If others accept
the spirit and methods of tact, family concord is possible.
Every instance of a good transaction increases the probabilities, raises the stock average!

Let's look at a pro.

A man hurried down the sidewalk. Out of a door came
another. They collided. Man Two blew up and showered
Man One with abuses.

Our hero smiled and said, "Mister, I don't know which
of us to blame. And I'm in too much of a hurry to investi-
gate. So, if I ran into you, I beg your pardon. If you ran
into me, don't mention it."

Still smiling, he walked away.

It's not just how you feel.
It's also what you say.
It's not only what you say.
It's the way you say it.

It's not always only what you can do.

It's how you do it.

Your home can be grand or a grind. The choice is in your hands, and those of your family.

Each hand has a touch. Make yours expert and fine. It's no less than required.

3
Watch Out for the Pendulum!

Mankind has progressed by alternations between extremes. So there is no point condemning left or right, conservative or liberal, saving or spendthrift, industry or inertia. Each has its place.

Yet, in a figure of speech, the pendulum suggests radical reactions. We tend to swing back and away from radical powers and ideas.

Examine the work of the pendulum in family life, and you hear:

My Dad was so strict with me, I'm going to be lenient with my children!

Our family had its fill of church, so I'm against forcing religion on kids.

My folks were so square, they wouldn't allow any liquor; believe me, we're keeping it in the house, and teaching our youngsters it's no sin to drink.

We were always off to some meeting or other! I'm done with all of that. We don't want to get involved.

So one extreme encourages its opposite. The pendulum swings, and produces excesses in attitude and practice.

It's helpful to know *the level* on which this thing

works—it is in the intestinal—the "gut" feelings. A person is full "up to here" with a certain kind of style, so out bursts an emotional response—a reaction based on glandular reaction.

One excess can do as much mischief as the other.

It's up to you to decide about things on the basis of how they *really* are, not only on how you emotionally react.

There are many aids to help us make choices:

psychology,
 history,
  statistics,
   ethics,
    morality,
     consideration,
      common sense, and
       faith.

These fields all suggest parts of the body higher than the intestines—touch, heart, ears, eyes, and brain!

All of them are superior to how you feel in "ulcer territory."

After all, right and wrong do not depend on what's been done and how it affected you, but on what is real, what is best.

So ride the pendulum away from one extreme.

But hop off before you swing to the other!

4
Freedom Inside Walls

I want to be free!
I want to be free!!
I WANT TO BE FREE!!!
I wAnT To bE FREe!!!!
So rocks the desperation of man, woman, boy, girl.
Everybody yearns to be without chains and walls.
—Especially around the house.
Free?
But what does it mean—to be free?
Here are two views on personal liberty:

People at your house should move free. They are clan-members, but also persons. Each one should pursue happiness the way he wants to. LET FREEDOM RING!

The people at your house should have it their way, but only if they injure nobody else. The freedom bell can't ring if it is cracked with self.

These opposites jell into one whole: All free places have boundaries. Independent people depend—upon one another.

Your house of peace is on stormy acres if even one member takes over on his terms. A tour through three homes tells why:

HOME 1 — "I'LL SAY WHAT'S ON MY MIND"

Here are Dad, Mom, seven children.

Nine people face the challenge to make this place a home.

Their unframed motto:

IF YOU THINK IT, SAY IT!

"You'd better come over here before the roof flies off!"

It's Betty calling me. They're having a rhubarb. It began over some bills, but now it's words-versus-words.

I walk into their DMZ.

Bob's having a drink in the kitchen, adding alcohol to his fire. Betty's enjoying an indignant cry.

The kids are embarrassed. As I enter, their faces glued to a TV unspectacular, they just say "Hi," rolling their eyes in my direction.

(Sometimes it's amazing how outstanding people slip into such ruts!)

Here's a fun family, when they're having a good day. They can raise the roof with great times. Everybody admires them—a beautiful bunch—when they pile into their wagon on the way to church. People ask Betty, "How do you do it?" What a tribe!

But few people suspect what eruptions come from these prettied-up fighters. At the foundation, there's one big crack: they are careless with speech.

You cannot say what you want, and keep harmony. Unlimited freedom of speech is a deception, a curse. Whatever you tell, expect to wound, if you don't use curbs on words that hurt. The use of

manners,

tact,
    consideration,
    politeness,
with a respectful tone of voice, delivers the best of you.

HOME II — "I" TROUBLES

Individualism is a strong human factor. As Unamuno said, "There cannot be another 'I'." Each of us has a "bubble of being." What we feel in our "bubbles" will be different from others.

In a sense, the bubble also represents privacy—the privilege of enjoying one's self, exclusively. Good "family" calls for this as a requirement with possessions, letters, time, clothing, etc.

And the bubble may stand for adventure. Here, you leave the beaten tracks and refuse to be mob-bound. Someone put it, "Don't keep forever on the public road, going only where others have gone."

So individualism has its values.

But when it becomes "bachelor," self-contained, non-community, personal isolation leads family people to egotism. It is "all for one," but seldom "one for all."

Your family relationships are affected by

    ✪ how often you use self-centered language,

    ✪ how much you are involved with others at home,

    ✪ and whether your demands exceed your concerns.

You are important as a person, but you are one among others, who, in the ideal family, love you, need you, serve you, want you. To return all this, is basically reasonable.

HOME III — "I'M ON MY OWN NOW!"

This is the first line of many a tragic ballad.

Lana was a slim blonde beauty. All clothes looked expensive on her. She had been trained in ballet, piano, and drama. Her IQ was so high, she was an intellectual charmer.

Sometimes she winced when teachers called her a brain.

Then she met Guv (from Governor, a nickname he had earned in Memphis, when he was class president). Guv was unshakable. He took every evening. He monopolized her.

And he demanded her body.

Guv's line was that sex should be free; the new morality had arrived. "Why hang onto Puritan taboos?"

What Lana missed somewhere was that true love is becoming a channel to bring joy to others. Guv wanted love for what it did for *him*.

Lana staged full revolt against the rules of her magnificent folks. In time she and Guv ran away, and lost contact with home.

She had freedom because she grabbed it like an apple and ran.

Months went by; she became addicted to narcotics. Her folks found her when she was critically ill. They carried her down three stair levels from her Village "pad."

Months later, Lana learned that her freedom had had a subtle bondage to it. She dressed her own way—yet she didn't; she looked like all her friends. She did what she wanted to, but the waste of time and talent made her feel guilty—another form of non-freedom.

She was independent, but knew her folks lay awake nights, worrying.

"I'm on my own now," is good, if it means maturity. The same sentence is tragic if it means swinging wild.

———◄●►———

These freedoms are all but free. Their costs mount up in
    actual financial outlay,
       suffering,
          emotional and mental illness,
             divorce,
                drunkenness, alcoholism, drug addiction,
                and worse.

When anybody demands irresponsible liberty, somebody always foots the bill. Relatives and friends, and sometimes the community and nation, pay the high cost.

Not so free!

One of the earliest Christians wrote at least two letters to his friends. In one of them, he advises,

> Live as free men; not however as though your freedom were there to provide a screen for wrongdoing . . . (I Peter 2:16 NEB).

No family can survive very long if its people play games with freedom. Let's lay down the limitations. Nobody can be free to

1. Be unkind, rude, thoughtless, or cruel.
2. Use other people to obtain what he's after, without their consent.
3. Satisfy his appetites at the expense of others.
4. Be dishonest.
5. Destroy the reputation, character, or well-being of another.

6. Take or molest the property of anybody else.
7. Say what he pleases, under every circumstance.
8. Cause worry or concern for other people.
9. Show disrespect for the good in others.
10. Be unpredictable, capricious, or irresponsible in conduct.

Family joy shudders to a stop when these breaches are made.

Here's the safest rule: When thinking of freedom for somebody else, pour it on generously. Let it flow over. Do it again.

But test your motives when you seek liberty for yourself. Ask whom you might injure; see if you *should* be free; look down the track of consequences.

Then reduce your own demands as much as you can. If other members of your family act this way, too, you've got it made.

———————

Inside your home, help every member to jangle easily. Common speech should not be challenged, nor action discouraged.

But your house has doors to walk through, walls to divide, furnishings to respect, and arrangements made for each person's needs.

These point to the kind of human order that cannot wait.

Others want independence, usually, as much as you. But every encounter and relationship calls for following *the rule*.

And the name of that rule is *LOVE*.

5
Why People Goof

No fence runs between normal people and the other kinds—no posts, no wires, nothing. We are all in the same corral.

Again, no time-line separates fumble-years from possible perfect days ahead.

We conjugate mistake-making:

I have goofed.	You have goofed.	He has goofed.
I goof.	You goof.	He goofs.
I shall goof.	You shall goof.	He shall goof.

On our up-days, we may see other people's faults 20-20. When we're down, we hope nobody's watching. But imperfection is built in. Everybody drops the cake sometimes.

When it comes to peace—family happiness, there are two types of behavior:

One leads to getting along—effective judgment.

The other brings on trouble between persons—the goof!

Double good comes from knowing this now.

First, it helps us learn why we have performance dips— we understand better what we see in the mirror.

Second, we learn better how to "read" others. Folks are not only bad or good—nice or difficult. Instead— *power-forces work deep beneath personality.* We may not be able to deal with them even when we know they exist. If we discover these elements, it doesn't rate us a doctorate in psychology. Or medicine. "A little learning is a dangerous thing." And sometimes we could be mistaken. But to understand options in behavior patterns broadens our tolerance. We improve the way we "handle" situations.

So, why do people goof? Have a glimpse of human frailty: try the four S's.

THE FIRST S—SICKNESS

Dotty began to be irritable. This was their first clue, because everyone knew her as the brightest gal in town— steady smile, stimulating wit. Her mother liked to tell people Dotty was the family balance-wheel.

Her brother first noticed she was "different." Then the family began to record her miscues. "Something's eating that girl," said her Dad.

They hadn't noticed Dotty's coordination began to fail—not at first, that is. She began to sway. She knocked over things anybody could see.

One day she went to her doctor, without telling the folks. The verdict was a life sentence: multiple sclerosis!

The family was shocked—then began to make up for their impatience. They wrote an inspiring chapter of courage, the way they handled Dotty's long confinement.

To sum it up, Dotty was committing one error after another. But she was *ill*.

———————◆•━━━━━━━

When you consider human complications, it's a wonder anybody keeps well.

Physically we are walking miracles.

There's a big word working for us when we have health: *homeostasis*. It refers to all the balances that keep us alive: temperature, blood pressure, bacteria-count, and those minute areas like the inner ear where we maintain equilibrium.

Or, think of the fluid between the iris and lens of our eyes that must flow just right, or they become cloudy.

If our physiques are that delicate, how impressively more complex are other factors:

      Mental   Emotional   Nervous

And illness may be in any one, or any combination of the four. *One usually affects the other.*

So you have discovered somebody else is ill? Maybe you have it right, maybe not.

But watch for this subtle dodge: Somebody has flipped a situation. You are convinced it's sickness. *You will be tempted to write him off.* "Oh, he's sick!"

He could be.

But by saying so, you may be reaching for one-upsmanship. You plaster the "sick" label like a semi-pro, and that's that. This could be a false judgment. But even if it's true, it tends to make you seem competent; he's the other way.

The red lights flash brighter when the sickness is *emotional*. If Sam has a broken leg, we "understand." We even write graffiti on his cast! But if Sam is down with anxiety, it's harder to be objective.

A case of nerves doesn't contain an ounce of sense. But when you have that kind of trouble, it's real. Some people can't even face the public, because they go to pieces. It's agony for them. They wish they weren't that way.

The factors of illness fill encyclopedias and hospitals. Persons may be *insane, sick, emotionally off,* or *nervous.* They are to be understood by those who are *sane, healthy, balanced,* and *steady.*

So ask about health, when people act up.

THE SECOND S—SINFUL

This is not a religious topic altogether.

Sometimes the goof could be just moral or ethical—serious enough.

And it may not be always the evil of one person. His wrongdoing could be the "sin" of the culture around him. So he is the product of a wicked community.

Many folks could make better, if it weren't for their neighborhood.

They've had training in foul play.

Whether it's heredity or environment, this person is off track. He does evil, and doesn't care. Sometimes the misdemeanors are light, but bothersome as a hangnail. But again he could go in so deep, he ranks criminal. Laws of society breathe down his neck.

He is in bad, bringing sorrow all around.

But what is the difference between this sinner and the sick one?

The answer is clear. Sick people err because they

have *infirmity*. They can't help acting the way they do—not usually.

But the sinner *means* it. Sin is any willful wrongdoing in the sight of God or man.

How to convert him depends on your denomination. What turns faith on in some people shuts it off in others.

The universal remedy is *a redeeming attitude*. The sinner has to come home.

Pick up stones?

"There, but for the grace of God, goes you?"

Forgiveness is an unblocked road for the stray. It can't be denied. Maybe the church—or the faith—or the clergyman—or a believing layman—can show the love needed. Preaching is advice that only can be heard by attractive actions.

Sin is counter-healing. It is one of the reasons people goof.

✐ THE THIRD S—STUPID ✐

The word is a bit strong; it was chosen for alliteration!

Stupid should be kept in the word-bank, brought out only for excessive situations.

Generally foolish behavior is seen as poor discernment—weird decisions, shaky judgment. Everybody has this kind of streak, much too persistent at times.

And dull-wittedness often surfaces without warning. Jerry Lewis once put it, after a not-so-funny *faux pas,*

Sinners can convert, but stupid is forever.

Ever say, "Now why did I *do* that?"

Sometimes a breach of common sense can be rationalized. It may even be tolerated, if we hold onto the other sense—*humor*. Rowdy fun can transform a prince into a spoof. Some of the best comedians in literature are stupid in a way. If everybody played every hand straight, the monotony would turn us gray.

But the habitual practice of poor judgment adds up tragedies. Maybe it is the problem of IQ. Or, it could be childish pride that refuses advice. Some won't learn from experience. They go from failure to failure, and family success declines.

Mike ———, fifteen, was described by his first-grade teacher as "adventuresome." His second-grade teacher had other words for it. To be frank about it, Mike would try anything once for curiosity, mischief, or spite.

He wore a path to the principal's office.

"Boys will be boys," as they say, but there is no substitute for common sense.

So Mike was a steady smoker when he was twelve.

And nipping whisky with a friend at fourteen.

There wasn't anything he wouldn't try. His parents knew he would do many things on a dare, but they felt he would outgrow all this.

Then, one day he went home with a chum who had gotten "high" by sniffing glue. Mike went for it, hand and claw.

Today, Mike's brain is irreparably damaged, and he will need custodial care the rest of his life.

So what was Mike's problem? One person might call him wicked, a bad boy, another say he was sick from the beginning. But somehow, even from the first, he was

plagued by the tendency to ignore the smart decision.
What to do?

Education could help, if we could corral people long
enough to teach them. Preaching has a spotty record for
being effectual. Encouragement and understanding never
go out of style.

Whatever the age of the judgment-offender, one course
must be taken: Live with him, so as to bring out his
highest potential.

Parents of retarded children know this better than anyone else.

The family as a *loving community* must support its
members, so that sensible decisions will be preferred.
Then, many of the wounds of erratic behavior will be
avoided.

THE FOURTH S—STUBBORN

This quality can be so refined it becomes heroic. Edison
and other committed scientists maintained their courses.
They wouldn't settle for anything until they had tried
everything they knew. Civilized stubbornness is

- a nurse staying by an injured patient,
  - a businessman keeping the company alive against
    many odds,
    - a teacher slugging it out with delinquency in
      a classroom.

So stubbornness has a famous first cousin, *determination*.

But unrefined, you have a criminal. He's without re-
gard or pity, cooperation is alien, and consideration of
other people a casualty.

Enter Sharron.

She's sixteen, at odds with her Mom (so typical, you know a case like this). Sharron is always right, and her mother, never. Open rebellion and arguing rock the air. But meanwhile, Sharron is a "pro" in making things hurt.

(Once more—what is this? Is Sharron sick? Sinful? Stupid? Or is she self-willed, bull-headed? Whatever the diagnosis, she's chock-full of *self*.)

So she uses every trick in the bag. One of her favorites is *procrastination*. Whatever could be done today, she puts off till tomorrow, if ever. A five-minute chore takes an hour. Some vital things are delayed so long, they spawn arguments and tiffs. But Sharron is never wrong. Her mother, she says, always bugs her.

At least, that's how it runs with the disputes. Humility and stubbornness are enemies. So Sharron never admits her mother has a point—always demands the last word, true or false, kind or cruel.

We seldom know how to deal with stubborn folks, because they are unpredictable. They call the shots; they set the course of the "game." The only winning methods are to be positive and patient, wiley and wise.

Whatever the problem with some member of your family (yourself too?) watch for one or more of the four S's. People off-base could be

SICK—SINFUL—STUPID—STUBBORN

Of course, this outline is not all the story. If it were, we'd simply call

● the physician for the sick,

   ● the preacher for the sinful,

● the teacher for the stupid,
   ● the policeman for the stubborn!

The FOUR s's at work will be revealed in following pages—but hold tightly to *hope*.

Nine most encouraging words:

> *No one needs to stay the way he is!*

6
Playing Top Pigeon

Animal experts have lots to tell us about ourselves. The "pecking order" in some birds reveals human traits! Pigeons in their pens play "King of the Hill," jousting for position.

One bird may be chief for awhile. But if he has a challenger, he may be pecked down to a lower rung.

Then he becomes subordinate and endures the ignominy of having surprises drop on his head!

It is the same as the "put down" people try on each other.

The story of the Prodigal Son paints a typical picture.

At the beginning, the father governed his house. Not a domineering Dad at all, he gave in when Junior decided to "cop out."

As he left, the Prodigal was temporarily "top pigeon."

He judged his home and family, and decided he wanted none of them.

He was sure he knew what to do with his share of the family fortune.

He also decided where he wanted to go, and couldn't care less about how chores would be done.

So off he went to the wild city, where he lost his "feathers." When he struggled home, he was voluntarily *down* in the pecking order.

> I will arise and go to my father, and will say unto him, Father, I have sinned against heaven, and before thee, and am no more worthy to be called thy son: make me as one of thy hired servants. (Luke 15:18, 19) .

But when he returned home, his elder brother made his try for the top rung. He whined to his father:

> Lo, these many years do I serve thee, neither transgressed I at any time thy commandment: and yet thou never gavest me a kid, that I might make merry with my friends: But as soon as this thy son was come, which hath devoured thy living with harlots, thou hast killed for him the fatted calf. (Luke 15:29-30)

This peeve was cut short by the kindly, understanding Dad:

> Son, thou art ever with me, and all that I have is thine. It is meet that we should make merry, and be glad; for this thy brother was dead, and is alive again; and was lost, and is found. (Luke 15:31-32)

So the rightful head of the house summed it up, and revealed his strength. Neither of the boys achieved mastery; it belonged to Dad.

———————•◦•———————

The modern scene officially still clings to the idea of "father at the top."

We say he's the head of the family, in a natural situation. He's the chief earner. He is physically stronger. He usually has a bigger voice. He gives the home his name. We list the family with "Mr." first.

But there are many examples of challenge.

Often the wives take over.

Why?

1. *They also hold jobs, enter professions, and sometimes earn as much as, even more than, their husbands.* Women's liberation!

2. *Women are often away from home as much as their husbands.* So many men need to put on gingham aprons.

3. *Women frequently have to manage* if their husbands
♣ lack enough personality or character,
♣ are addicted to alcohol or dope,
♣ are crippled or chronically ill, or
♣ have serious emotional or mental problems.

4. *Women own more than they ever have.* "It's a man's world" is old hat now.

5. *Women widowed by death or divorce must take over as heads of familes.*

So being on top depends on various factors. Dad may be the happy monarch of the house. Yet the scepter may shift from time to time.

The biggest concern is this: if anyone is at the top, it should be on the basis of the situation, not playing games. Then authority is handed *up* by the rest of the family, and is not usurped by force or fury.

Occasionally newsmen reveal the discovery of a sick family situation.

In one home, a widowed mother decided the world was too wicked for her children. So she boarded them up for seven years in a filthy room. Food, books, and clothing were slipped to them through a small crack.

Any pastor could tell of discovering homes where a pushy dad has gone to seed on his paternal rights.

Sometimes mental illness shows up in his wife.

Children may be abused.

Then there's the beloved but autocratic Aunt Hattie or Grandpa Jack who means well, but who rules by emotion.

These people know how to use tears and threats to work things out their way.

And finally, youthful revolts are bids by teen-agers to take the upper perch.

In the early 1920s, the Duke of Windsor, then the Prince of Wales, said that the amazing thing about the United States was the way parents here obey their children. For decades we felt we should concentrate on service and attention to youth. But something made that cake fall.

On many a family roost, the teen-ager has become top pigeon, and it's unpalatable. He demands money, clothes, entertainment, the car, and freedom to make decisions, but he's not ready to be independent.

Is the "youth problem" any surprise?

———————•◆•———————

"Dominate" and "domineer" are related to the Scottish *dominie,* the name given to the schoolmaster or the pastor.

It means he has superior knowledge, maturity, and control. The Scots obtained the word from the Latin *dominus,* meaning "lord."

The question should be asked, "Must your home have a lord?"

In a sense, YES. One parent or the other or, better still, both parents, should assume this posture. They have the "divine right."

But it is held in jeopardy, because it must be validated through the years by:

1. *Humility.*

Being lords, they also *have* a lord. For Christian homes that lord is Jesus Christ. For Jewish homes, it is Jehovah. And in homes where religion has had little or no mention, there must still be principle that provides the chart and compass.

2. *Consistency.*

Remember Sherlock Holmes, and what he told his colleague? "Good old Watson!" he said. "You are the one fixed point in a changing world."

Parents cannot be like rudderless rabbits on an open prairie. They must know their beliefs and convictions, and stick to them.

Children may reject what you worship, but never mind! Better to teach and be ignored than not to have directions.

3. *Integrity.*

The thing that brought the Prodigal back home wasn't just being hungry. He knew that his father was to be trusted as loving and forgiving.

Children, without knowing it, are constantly testing

to see what we are. Like Will Rogers, they are looking for "the real bird."

4. *Expertise.*

The ability to lead is not produced in a vacuum.

Leaders know something. Some people's judgment seems instinctive. They appear to have it naturally.

Others have read books, gone to conferences, been faithful in church, and have stored up resources.

There are skills and strategies that masters must have; if they don't, leaders must get them or fail.

Many parents have told me, "Pastor, I just don't know what to do."

5. *Patience.*

People at the top keep their cool. They aren't stampeded by a dented fender.

6. *Hope.*

Sometimes when parents do their best, their children turn out their worst. But the master can't give up. He tries hard and lets whatever unseen good there is take the rest.

A famous painting shows Faust and the Devil playing chess, and the chess pieces are in the position of checkmate. The Devil is going to win this game. But a man looked at the picture for a long time, then finally spoke out, "It's a lie! It's a lie! The king and knight have another move!"

Often the parent who thinks he's failed is saved by hope. The king and the knight have another move.

———◆●◆———

So much for those who should rightfully rule. But what about the culprits—

❂The Domineering Dad,

❂The Matriarchal Mom,

❂The Grandiose Grandparents,

❂The Tough Teen-agers,

❂The Kooky Kids?

When they try to reverse the pecking order, what should the masters of the situation do?

1. *Size it up.* The diagnosis may give you a shock, but you shouldn't avoid it.

What is this whip-cracker trying to do?

Why?

What's behind his drive for superiority?

Is he inferior? Angry? Hurt? Hostile?

Then, what brought it all on?

2. *Seek an outside counselor.* Discuss the problem with him first; maybe later he can sit in with you as you have a family caucus.

I have found that usually the person who sees the need comes with the complaint.

Next I visit the offender.

Third, we have a three-way pow-pow, and the crisis is met. Sometimes you multiply this process by three or four, because many problems are too sticky for a one-time approach. Often I have been a referee over many years!

3. *Have a chat.* More educated people would say, "Go into dialogue." However you put it, conversation is it—

not pouting, shouting, bouting, touting, or flouting! Get a good book on how to conduct a bull session.

This process should begin early. The longer you wait, the harder it is to do it!

4. *In extreme cases, take extreme measures.* Sometimes the dictator won't budge himself, and has to be budged. "To budge or not to budge?" That *is,* for sure, the question.

If the "budge" means finding another home, this is serious surgery, and should be considered only as the last resort.

If it means forced diagnosis and therapy, this too is traumatic. Know what you're doing.

I've had to assist a judge and a doctor in administering sedatives in forced commitment to a mental hospital. These are extreme and tragic cases.

When people are reasonable, there's hope for working out life together in charity and common sense. In this case, nobody tries to be top pigeon. That's game-playing.

Family life is too complex and so precious that nobody should attempt to make it a game to try to come out the "winner."

Mature goals show each person respected for what he is.

Then everybody, meaning the family, wins at peace.

7
Tell It Like (As) It Is

If homes can have heart trouble, it's in this area: *the problem of truth-telling.*

The symptoms open with a sharp pain when a lie has surfaced, and are followed by days and nights of heartache.

Sin has many tools, but a lie is the handle that fits them all.

One spring day, I came home and found termites near the side door. At once I applied an insecticide, and felt I had defeated the invader. Later, signs began to appear that they were back again. So we called the exterminators!

Months after, we found areas where mischief had been done, and repair bills mounted.

No home can survive for long under the invasion of falsehoods. They attack trust, love, concern—all the rafters and joists of the home.

Here are examples of the lie at work:

∾ૡ૰· **|** ·ૡ૰∾

HUSBAND TO WIFE: One Monday, June called me. "He's at it again," she wept.

Business was heavy that November—early Christmas rush.

Max had hired extra help.

He fussed about hard work all the way to the bank. Sunday morning.

"I've got to go to the shop."

June accepted it naturally, though later she admitted her ESP was beginning to churn.

About 10:30 (this wasn't really acting on suspicion, June assured me) she thought of some items she needed from the store, and called. *No answer.* At 11:00, the same.

So she climbed into the VW to see what had gone wrong.

Max's car was in front of the Skadmires'. Mrs. S. was a divorcée with two children. June drove on.

He came home at noon. "Man! Statements have piled up—everything's short on the shelves—the shop's a mess!"

June cried, "Max, I *know* where you were this morning!"

Moments of silence.

"I spent some time over at Van's—now don't get excited—nothing went on—the poor kid needed advice on some problems—I just went over and talked with her— you know how I love you, don't you, June?"

ᴏᴥᴏ· **‖** ·ᴏᴥᴏ

WIFE TO HUSBAND: At the hairdresser's, my wife overheard this: "Well, Tommy wanted an odometer for his bike. His dad said no. So I took some of my grocery money and bought it. Then I told Tom to be sure to keep the bike where his dad wouldn't see it."

Let's guess that Tommy's father may have been difficult about money, and too strict for understanding. This is often the way of it.

But Tommy's mother was tampering with a vital appliance in the house of peace—*the mutual need for trust.*

So, man or woman, Adam or Eve—the lie degrades; dishonesty is our worst side.

∾✌· **III** ·✌∾

CHILDREN TO PARENTS: Rank this high on the list.

(*Homework for moms and dads:* How do you help children to be truthful?)

It can start very young: "I didn't do it, Mommy" can be the beginning of a lopsided career. If it becomes habitual, you need help to find out why.

Probably every child has lied to his parents sometime.

But if teen-agers deceive Mom and Dad to cover misdemeanors, parents ask how to cope with it.

Some resort to scolding, threats, and punishments. These do the job sometimes, with some youngsters.

But probably there are no substitutes for example, patience, and an occasional family lesson on honesty. Your parable could be on trying to make bread without following the recipe—or how the car motor will fall apart if the mechanic fails to put cotter pins on the bolts. So, "Honest people are healthier, happier, safer, etc. . . ."

(And you know that this might turn them *on* or *off*—who can tell?)

But for now, dishonest kids make uneasy parents.

And did I mention *example?*

Then, how about

IV

PARENTS TO CHILDREN: Here's the sticky one!

Back in German II, we had to be able to tell this story, *auf Deutsch:*

> One day a father and his son went walking. Suddenly, the boy said, "Father, yesterday I saw a dog as big as a horse!"
>
> At first the father answered nothing.
>
> Later, however, the father spoke to his son, saying, "Son, soon we are coming to a bridge, and whoever has told a lie, falls on that bridge and breaks a leg."
>
> Quickly the son spoke again, "Father, that dog was only as big as a cow."
>
> Then they came into sight of the bridge, and the boy cried out, "Father, that dog was only as big as a calf."
>
> Finally, they arrived at the bridge. The boy stopped short.
>
> "Why don't you come?" asked the father.
>
> "Father," came a trembling voice, "that dog wasn't any bigger than *our* dog!"

The moral was clear, but the backlash erased it. The lad was frightened into giving it straight.

But what will the *father* do when the boy discovers his dad's whopper?

So parents pile up debts in fibs about Santa Claus, the Easter Bunny, and how babies come. The credibility gap widens when children discover the deceptions!

Much more serious are deliberate falsehoods.

Once, when a father was badly injured in a car wreck,

the family shielded the little daughter by playing his suffering down.

Parents often deceive children as to *the reasons why we do some things,* or why not.

There may be extenuating circumstances, but all adults know they take up serious business when they try to con their children. They can bear more truth than we think.

———————•••———————

Nobody—absolutely nobody—can compel you or me to be truthful. It's an inside job—it depends upon what we want, what motivates us.

8
When the Fuse Blows

Sometimes family lights go out.

The telephone jangled a Saturday afternoon SOS. I hurried to a suburban home.

Karen had phoned from Oklahoma; she was married. Her high school senior class would graduate in a month. We didn't know if she was in a family way (she wasn't).

Her dad was ready to blow his new son-in-law's head off, when they returned. Her mother was hysterical.

But Kevin, Karen's older brother, couldn't see why all the fuss. He was out of sorts with his folks.

They couldn't understand his detachment from *l'affaire*.

Sum it up in tears: a once-peaceful family was in turmoil. There was lots of adjusting before calm was possible again—

A few other cases have records of bringing on crises:

★Disagreements about money, property, or wills.

★Dislike for some new in-law member of the family.

★Too much parental nagging.

★Teen-agers breaking family rules.

★Trouble in school, with grades, teachers, other pupils.

★Husband-wife lack of harmony.

★A "hassle" over religion.

So, as we say, the fuse blows.

———————◆◆———————

One night the Two-by-Two young marrieds of my church planned a waffle supper. The girls prettied up the church basement till it looked like a Manhattan cafe.

We men were going to do all the cooking.

Anticipation was under pressure.

So, out in the kitchen, we had dirtied every dish and spoon (that's men!). If the batter had been mortar, we could have built a new church. Syrup (three kinds) was in table pitchers. Real butter glistened gold on each table. Coffee was made, simmering in eighty-cup perks.

The waffles must be done just before serving. "Have the blessing first," said Eldon, "before we pour the first batter on." So grace was said.

In the kitchen, six waffle irons were plugged in at once.

That, plus the coffee urns, did it! The circuit was overloaded, all lights out. The most the lines would bear was two irons at a time!

"Oh well," said Gladys, "we'll just make the best of it!"

A parable: Family peace can bear just so much voltage. Its capacity may carry the normal run of daily wear and grind. But when high-wattage situations hit the circuit, there has to be more power to handle it, or the overloading must go.

Here are some unique approaches:

1. *Allow some time for emotional demonstration.* Too

often, when tragedy presses your doorbell, you want everybody to calm down, take it softly, avoid a stampede.

Why?

It's probably because you want to avoid heart attacks, apoplexy, or stroke!

Or maybe you just can't "stand to see a man cry," or people to emote over the brim.

Yet, one of the best ways to meet sudden sorrow is to *let go*. An open cry helps some people. Even an emotional expression of anger is helpful, when under control.

Sustained anger or hatred do much damage, but momentary releases of pent-up resentment can prevent inner catastrophe. Often it's the one with the unruffled face who has ulcers!

Nobody's proud to admit flying off the handle when peace is interrupted. But it's safer to slam a door than to burst blood vessels.

So let each one in the family have his emotional binge. But then let everybody get over it.

2. *After the emotional catharsis, do the immediate thing.* A phone call may be necessary, can't wait. A trip needs to be planned. If somebody's coming, there's dinner, room overnight, chores to do, people to see. Your first actions are down-payments on future chores.

3. *Take care of the people most immediately affected.* Louie, young father of three children, was a top-rung radio announcer—man of many talents. He moonlighted through many a dance at the drums so he could meet house payments, medical bills, etc.

One night his wife Lynda called her folks. Louis had been picked up for selling dope.

Her parents got into their car, drove the fourteen miles. Lynda needed support and understanding. They did what they could to love her.

Then they turned to Louie. They arranged a visit with him in the county jail, engaged an attorney, consulted a physician.

They set in motion everything that could work for Louie's restoration.

Next they visited Louie's employers at the radio station, some of his friends, a neighbor or two, and their pastor.

All this—but first, they turned helping hands toward Louie's family and Louie!

4. *Don't overdo.* You can't control hard luck. It would be great if you could. A certain amount of it is good for everybody. If you shield people from it, you could deprive them of the benefits of *struggle.*

You might want to take over, but this hints they aren't strong or wise enough to manage themselves. Probably it's best to do only what the persons affected can't.

Even then, it ought to be with their consent. People can get terribly upset if even the best-intended aid is forced upon them.

5. *Help everybody concerned to get over it.* A blown fuse is a temporary crisis. Like all trouble, it could cause lasting harm. But the original cause itself is an emergency, and rates treatment as such. It takes mature people to say "This too shall pass . . ."

You can't prevent tragedies from knocking at your door, but you don't need to feed them.

You may have a heartful of religion and faith, but panic when the circuits are shorted.

Best decide now how you will act when the roof caves in.

Remember the old Scot on his deathbed?

His daughter offered to read him a chapter.

"No, daughter," he replied, "that won't be necessary. The storm's up now. I thatched my roof in calm weather."

Some of us are braced like that.

Most of us need to be.

Then we'll have extra fuses around when the systems are overloaded.

9
Sometimes Religion Divides

Religious difference disrupt some families. I have spent many pastoral years trying to reconcile people who should be united by their faith, not divided.

There is some hope. Bridges from church to church are being engineered. An air of cordial acceptance prevails. We are in league now, more than ever. Joint prayer books, hymnals, and study-texts have been published. Speakers and preachers exchange platforms. Reconciliation is in the mill.

Yet, many families are divided over *spiritual* matters. Several studies have shown that mixed marriages fail about twice as often as marriages within one faith.

It is difficult to forsake a religion practiced since childhood. Even when a man may have never "gotten with" his church, he may refuse to accept another. Sometimes, he doesn't know what his affiliation means or what his church teaches.

A little girl filled out a questionnaire in school. For her religion, she wrote "Baptist." Her teacher knew she wasn't any such thing, and asked her about it. She replied, "I am really a Presbyterian, but I can't spell it!"

In other cases, there are, however, intelligent preferences. Take two or more people who believe they are the only ones headed for heaven, and the fat sizzles.

And occasionally we face the question of intellecutal integrity.

A man came to my study, distraught. His wife belonged to a tiny church of a minority sect.

At their wedding, the pastor's wife "prophesied" that the couple would never bear children. When pregnancy was diagnosed, the lady convinced the church the man's wife was *not* expecting. When the child was born, she told the church it had been adopted, because the Lord had told her they would have no child, and *you cannot go against the word of the Lord.*

This happened in the U.S.A., in 1970!

Other instances may not be so shocking, but a divided family is a divided family.

The big question arises, "What will we do about religion?" when people come from differing backgrounds. Let's consider each possibility:

1. *Drop church altogether.*

This is the path of least resistance, the choice of desperation.

So Sundays are spent doing chores, shopping, following hobbies, or sleeping in. Religion is usually avoided in conversation.

Things may go smoothly for a time, but there are days when decisions must be made. They are:

✪feast days,

◉crucial events, like weddings or funerals,
◉and when there are children to rear.

Many parents who have sloughed off religious activity at the first of marriage return to it at one of these times.

Then there are the unexpected developments, after marriage.

A father called me. He had been a faithful Methodist, his wife a Lutheran, but she had recently converted to a sect that condemned Christmas as a feast day.

She would allow no gifts for the four children, no carol-singing, no Christmas tree. So the father dropped all religious connection rather than face the conflict.

Statistics favor religious observance by both husband and wife. The largest number of marriage failures occur among the nonreligious. That is why it is important to find a better solution than quitting. The options follow:

2. *Each side follows its own faith.*

This can be done with much success. But you must add one more phrase: "—and is tolerant of the other's religion!"

There is much that faiths hold in common. Anyone holding to the major denominations can find exciting similarities. Even Christians and Jews may appreciate each other's rites and rituals.

It is helpful to view belief in God as a huge umbrella under which all people of faith may abide. For many, this is a "syncretic" idea, and not doctrinal enough.

But it faces the truth: most of us have inherited our beliefs. But for the "accident" of birth, we could have been in any of the other camps.

3. One of the two joins the other's faith.

This works sometimes, fails others. When either side moves over to the other, it is often true that he has been weaker in his faith than the other. But not always. He (or she) may simply assume that it is better to team up than go solo.

It is sad when radical orthodoxy takes over. A confirmed doctrinaire can be most difficult.

If anyone in the family changes over, it is not this one. Everybody else is on another network.

Though it is inspiring for people to be convinced about their church, family peace lives better in the spirit of tolerance. Henry Ward Beecher wrote:

> Beware of religious faiths that separate men. Beware of religious faiths that put forth a hand bearing a flail, and go into life beating down, beating down. . . . Look for those religious administrations that draw men together; that inspire good will; that teach patience and gentleness and forbearance.

Folks who believe like this will find it possible to celebrate their faith together. They sit down to the banquet and feast on the common gifts of religion.

All the rest sit around and pick the bones of orthodoxy.

4. They both leave their former churches, and find a new one.

Very good! But this warning: often this takes too long. I've known some who have been shopping for twenty years, and still are unsettled.

Their religion is Procrastination.

Better set a time, like three or four months, or weeks.

Finding a middle faith occurs usually with those from extreme rituals.

If a Baptist marries an Episcopalian, they usually reach toward the Congregational, Methodist, or Presbyterian.

If a Church of Christ member weds a Baptist, they may try the Disciples (Christian) Church.

And a Catholic who marries into an old-line Reformed family often settles for the Episcopal Church!

Such choices provide familiar elements for each, without complete surrender to the other's background.

The Bahai Temple in Wilmette, Illinois, is a parable in lacy stone. It has nine sides and is about the same height as the Taj Mahal. Near the top, the walls veer toward the center to form a pointed dome.

The Bahai faith teaches that there are nine principal religions in the world. As they reach toward God, however, they lose their separate identities.

You may not accept Bahai teachings, but the point rings well.

Many of our differences are the result of *history* and *personality*. As such, they have less bearing upon the substance of faith. But if most people could begin with *what religion is meant to be,* cooperation could be more possible.

Try this definition for now:

Religion is the attitude of a person toward a Supreme Power which regulates his own life and his relations with others.

All the creeds and dogmas, all the sacraments and rituals, are commentary to this one general summary.

When religion *divides,* it is usually at some minor point. Whenever it *unites,* more important factors have been held in focus.

———————●●●———————

But what if part of the family is *agnostic* or *atheistic?* First, it would help to separate the two.

The agnostic is one who *"does not know."* Either he has tried, and fails to understand, or has postponed the search.

"Not knowing," he remains inactive and unconvinced. In a sense, he is one with people of faith, because religious knowledge is not verifiable. There are many ways of "knowing."

Often the agnostic rejects religion because he does not learn *in his way.*

The atheist is more hard-core. He is convinced that there is no God, or, in more recent terms, that God is dead. He sees no point in believing in God, and often substitutes an ethical system to live by. He may accept humanism as the substitute for religion-based-on-God.

Strife in a family may result from the faith-member and the no-faith-member each trying to convince the other. How to turn people to God, or away from God, is a problem of *persuasion.*

That's the theme of the next chapter!

10
Trying to Manage Somebody?

"Clarence, don't you think it's about time to get ready?"

"Clarence, get washed for supper."

"Clarence, look at the mess you just left!"

"Clarence, I saw you speaking to Sam at the lodge meeting. What were you talking about?"

"Clarence, what are you doing now?"

"Clarence . . ."

Whenever A tries to manage B, tensions could tighten. It depends on B, and how he relates to A.

We'll grant it: some members of the family (like mother and father) should guide others (like children).

And sometimes an older member needs the help of younger ones.

Others—the citizens of encounter—face give-and-take in trying to influence without resentment.

There's no way of spelling out just how much A can expect B to do for him. It depends upon the amount of respect, or perhaps fear, that has been built up.

But if A continually pushes, B is almost sure to apply the brakes with, "When can I live my *own* life?"

However noble the cause for it, the relationship of "Boss and Bossed" is uncomfortable.

A has made himself judge. He knows. He has it made. Sometimes he's older, bigger, smarter, richer, or louder.

So, he pushes and suggests and commands.

Often he uses power methods.

In contrast, B is the one judged. He does not know. He is the loser, or the one who hasn't made it yet. Usually he's younger, smaller, has less education, is poorer or quieter.

So B is bugged by suggestions and "guidance."

———————

Let's visit the Craigs in Illinois. Mrs. Craig lives with her son John and family. She is devout, rich, and pushy.

Though there are many spots of irritation, the rawest is about church. John and Cathy stopped going to worship right after marriage.

So Mrs. Craig tries to wheedle them into a pew every Sunday. The more she coaxes, the more they balk. Church isn't their dish.

So here is the pattern: A dares to manage B.

In Colorado, Fred has been married to Marge twelve years, but enjoying it less.

Marge is lazy; her house is a jungle. Often, when Fred comes home from work, supper isn't even started, and Marge is dutchy and drab.

Fred is A. He has tried every method in the book to change Marge, B. Sometimes he gets loud, but it doesn't work. Marge hasn't changed, and the more he frowns, the more she winces.

Ellen and Eleanor are identical twins. Ellen was dating a boy with a reputation for failure. As Eleanor put it, "When he was in kindergarten, he even flunked in milk!" He was a high school dropout, a flop, and a bum. He lost every job he ever had. He wore grubbies, had revolting table manners, and shied away from all polite affairs.

Eleanor (A) was concerned over the future of her sister (B). How could she persuade her to break off? (In this case, A is trying to turn B off; it's no different—the game's the same.)

If A is "only trying to help"—you know, the sincere effort to guide and influence—the attempt sounds innocent. Even then he can irritate.

Nobody enjoys being taken over for management.

Sometimes, however, A could have *dubious reasons* for wanting to domineer. Maybe he is jealous, resentful, egotistic, or covets Top Pigeon satisfaction in controlling B.

Whatever the motivation, the heart of the solution is *understanding*.

Why does one person try to master another?

A primary reason for the attempt to guide another person is the *conviction that you have better perspective.*

The one whose conduct is in question, you feel, *doesn't realize what is happening to him.* You can see what he doesn't. Maybe he is so wrapped up in his situation that he doesn't sense the conditions. Maybe he is so young,
    so inexperienced,
      so busy,

so confused,
> or even so sick
he can't think for himself.

What usually happens, then, is the grab for control. Methods may be open or subtle, blunt or crafty. Sometimes the A people are geniuses in devising schemes. If you are an A-type, here are some of your most likely approaches:

1. *You may make open criticisms or suggestions.* This is taking liberties with anybody's heart.

A stands for *Authority.* Your experience, age, education, and endowment qualify you to take over. Sometimes you may cast yourself as judge and jury—even executioner! While such decisive action may be called for, your family now lives on Tension Terrace.

Of course, it is different between parent and child; we are dealing primarily with adult transactions.

2. *You may invite a friend in to take your side.* If so select him carefully! Make sure he's briefed on the need in advance.

Then, when you bring up a point (at dinner?) he won't turn Brutus on you.

It's bad strategy to trust untried spokesmen. You select the vocation wisely: a minister for religious opinion, a psychologist for behavior, a popular man-about-town for general subjects. Less formal, of course, is to enlist the help of a relative.

The point is to use a third party to put across what you can't.

3. You may drop subtle hints. This is well-worn strategy. Direct attack is too suspect. Beware if your prospect learns you're trying to be cagey. He'll resent it all the more, because you're taking him for a goose.

Once he knows you have tried the hint-bit, he'll become sensitive and touchy. Even when later you are not being sneaky, he will suspect you are. "Innocent you" will be resented.

4. You may write notes. Chit-writing has a checkered career. Tactful letters may help.

If overdone, or written by one who doesn't have status with recipient, they can make things worse.

The safest letters are expressions of praise, or thanks. Positive note-writing rarely fails. Backfire is scarce.

But when it carries advice, suggestions, sarcasm, or criticism, the note's not often the thing.

————◆•◆————

People try these techniques to influence one another. They all involve risk.

The line between being helpful and critical is paper-thin.

Your goal is *to be a helpful human.*

In the family, this extends to the desire for all others to be human, too. Thus, much care is needed if you're trying to *get to* somebody else.

One of the tightest tensions in every family is this:

> *How to grant each person his freedom,*
> *and at the same time help him be his best.*

If you seek superiority for another reason, examine your

motives. You take on serious business when you want to mold another.

The effort to rule may be attempted by adults, youths, or children who

✪are sincerely concerned, and want to help (*normal*) ;

✪are neurotic or psychotic, and domineer (*abnormal*) ;

✪are cruel; enjoy suppressing others (*sadistic*) . .

Parents are not suspect when they try to rear great children. But the day must come for them when they say, "We've finished our work. We've said our piece. We've given our examples . . . tried, coaxed, and prayed. Now it is up to them. Our children must now be on their own— set their courses, free from our directions."

That's healthy parenthood.

Sometimes the effort sours.

Many parents enjoy their little children, but as they come to age ten or so, the battle-points are set.

So in the early teens conflicts appear like mushrooms.

This very day I saw the first stages at a dime store.

A mother had three children along, the eldest about twelve. She begged her mother to buy sunglasses.

Her mother said, "No."

"But, Mother," whined the daughter. "All the other girls are wearing them!"

"No, Sue; I told you we are not going to buy them!"

Sue began to sulk. Later she sassed and put on a bad face. The fight was on.

And her mom, bless her, made NO mean NO.

Eventually, the teen-ager enters the adult world. Now

he stands almost as tall (maybe even taller) than his parents.

The tables often turn, and teens make their tries too. They themselves may begin to umpire somebody in the family.

I've seen a fourteen-year-old girl try to get her father to stop drinking.

So now it can be anybody—grandparent, uncle or aunt, parent, older youth, teen-ager—becoming A, the bold-molder.

Perhaps you are the one who is trying to call the plays.

Ask these questions:

Is this really for the good of the person you're working on?

Or is it for some selfish satisfaction? You've heard the matron on the detergent opera crying, "But Bellicent! I'm doing this for your own good! You can see that, can't you, dear?" Take that one to the judge!

It would require delicate surgery to dissect all personal concerns from a situation. Yet your motives are under test. Maybe your own reputation as a leader in the family is up for grabs. Perhaps you stand to lose money, or power, or favor, if you don't stop somebody.

Maybe you are trying to keep your ward under the home roof.

It might be better for him to relocate. But *you* would be lonely? Can *you* let go of selfish ambitions and desires?

Is there some chance it wouldn't be as bad as you think it would be, if you stayed out of it?

You might fear a major trend to the bad. Then when

specific things occur, matching this tendency, you panic? Mark this big: THE SMALLER THE POINT OVER WHICH YOU MAKE YOUR PLAY, THE MORE IRKSOME YOU'LL BE.

Avoid becoming vigilante. You are more likely to fail if you feel you must ride up and challenge all opponents.

You don't need to put out every brush fire, pull every weed, lock every gate.

Are you a good example?

This question has a sting to it. But really! Can your subject look to you with respect? You see, when you make yourself a mold, you have troubles in two ways:

If you aren't that good, you speak from a lower position—

but if you are too Grade A, your subject can resent you.

The one who tries to influence the other puts his example on the line.

> Big Sam was humble and quiet,
> And very slow of speech.
> But he touched the hearts of several
> His pastor couldn't reach,
> Because he lived the sermon
> He knew he couldn't preach.

Will you say more by speaking, or by doing? Think it over.

Are you willing to say your piece, then back off to leave it to your subject?

This is a toughy. You know that if you say too little, he may not get the point. But if you overkill, you'll lose him. Teen-agers especially complain about adults who "bug" them. Nobody enjoys someone constantly breathing down his neck.

There are times when things get out of hand. They rate extreme measures. Emergencies require action, with all the guidance you can secure. The lawyer, minister, judge, doctor; the organizations, clinics, friends—all stand ready to help.

But until a crisis arises, you may be facing the racket at home. Now you're the one in the slot who has to be responsibile.

If you put on the paper hat and try to be captain, expect to face the battle. Only experts may know when you've said it, when you've done it. Most of us aren't that gifted.

So, in dealing with crises, you make the comment you think best. You try to be easy to live with, and the best example you can. Let your genuine love show in how you look, act, and speak. Be firmly committed to doing your part in the family. Build up the general culture of understanding. Be loyal to each member. Put in your best effort.

Then, send a prayer up for everyone at the day's close. And that's about it.

Wendell Phillips, American orator and reformer, once said of Ralph Waldo Emerson, "If Emerson would go to hell, his presence there would surely change the climate."

This goes for all ambitious "controllers" in families. Be the kind of person who sets an encouraging tone.

Then you will help others enjoy being their best.

Ah, yes! If you're trying to manage someone, *you've* been reached somehow.

What turned you on?

11
Marriage and Divorce

It was the de-mating season.

Parting couples were queued up at all the counselors' offices in our town.

It's rough to dodge the flak of these frays. After all, strife is behind the decision. There are all the accouterments of war:

> battle lines,
>> attack,
>>> defense,
>>>> wounds,
>>>>> casualties,
>>>>>> division of spoils!

But it's even worse to realize the switch.

They stand before the altar. You see them at their prettiest, cleanest, happiest, and holiest. Money seems to be no object. Flowers and candles beautify the smiles of well-wishing guests.

Then here comes the bride!

The wedding party turns with her as she steps to the altar. Music has climaxed and ended. The congregation is seated. The minister begins with

> Dearly beloved, we are gathered
> together to join this man and this
> woman in holy matrimony . . .

Thus, the marriage clock is started. How long will it run—thirty years? Fifteen? Five? Less than a year?

Divorce can destroy these holy vows,
>   indicating the couple (or one of them) forgot,
>   failed in working out the domestic details,
>   found somebody else,
>   or were disappointed in the whole business.

Naturally, children are often caught in the cross-fire. They are not the "little rivets in the ship of matrimony" some romantics have tagged them.

> Between "Here comes the bride"
>   and "Here comes the judge,"
>   something distintegrates.

MARRIAGE SAYS:	DIVORCE REPLIES:
I love you	*I can't abide you*
We can make it together	*We won't try any longer*
To have and to hold	*To leave and forsake*
For better or for worse	*For better, but not for worse*
Till death us do part	*We can't wait that long*
We exchange rings in token	*We return the rings*
Whom God has joined	*Let man put asunder.*

Statistics? In 1967, the U.S.A. recorded 1,913,000 marriages. But with 534,000 couples, the dove of peace couldn't take it!

At 2:30 A.M., the doorbell shattered sleep.

Madge was on our front porch for the fifth time in a month. Steve had staggered in at two, stoned. He accused her of seeing another man, knocked her into a corner, then went to the kitchen for another drink. Madge escaped and sought asylum with us.

Here was a girl between.

Wedding memories and vows were still fresh, but befouling was underway. She was beginning to discuss divorce.

What should she do?

The answer begins with what she and Steve should have known at first. It may not help Madge to have 20-20 hindsight, but her experience marks rather common danger-points.

Look for four factors in marriage success. In more than thirty years of observing marriages, and in counseling nearly half a thousand couples, I have yet to see a marriage fail when these foundations are laid:

1—PARTNERS IN RELIGIOUS LIFE

Which comes first, chicken or egg? Are religious couples more able to cope with reality—or is it that realistic people decide to include religion? Whatever the case, the two track together.

Across the U.S.A., the present rate is about one divorce for three and one-half marriages.

But a poll was reported by Dr. Louis H. Evans, onetime pastor of Hollywood First Presbyterian Church, that *if Mr. and Mrs. are members of the same faith and work at it together, the ratio becomes a thin one-to-seventy!*

⚬⚬⚬· 2—UNDERSTANDING WHAT MARRIAGE MEANS ·⚬⚬⚬

This could be related to religion. That's because love and faith are brother and sister.

You cannot really deal with marriage without talking about love.

You can't talk religion and avoid mentioning love.

So people come to the altar for marriage. They confess they "love" one another. But what does that say?

In both marriage and religion, attitude tells all.

In either case, how one comes out will depend upon the entry. And the reason why religion is so vital, along with a psychological understanding, is this: *religion determines the kind of love in marriage.*

People may enter either faith or marriage for the wrong motives. If so, they become disenchanted—want to call the whole thing off. I have seen direct correlation between why some people leave the church and others cancel marriage vows.

It is found in the kind of love.

The Greeks and Latins had several words which have become "love" to us. Let us consider them, from the bottom up:

Epithamia.

You have to reach out for the connection, but this word represents a "form" of love. The New Testament translates it *lust* (I John 2:16, for instance). In many popular songs, movies, and plays, though, *epithamia* would be *love, love, love.*

The dead giveaway is that this "love" is given *only for what the giver gets out of it!*

Eros.

This is the name of the ancient Greek god of love. Cupid is his popular name.

Actually, here is an authentic form. It deals with *first exposures.* The fellow sees a girl on the midway at the fair, and they "hit it off." They make the rides, the sideshows, the games, and the races.

The transaction may end there, but this flirtation is vestibule to friendship, courtship, engagement, and marriage. It is often sensuous (erotic, erogenous), but not necessarily wicked. It's just that it is too shallow a base for marriage.

Couples shouldn't go from the midway to the parsonage!

Caritas.

The Latins come in for this one. From it, we have *charity.* We are advancing in the comprehension of love.

Sympathetic understanding is the key. The other person and his welfare are the object of your concern.

This, too, is a worthy concept. The ability to project yourself into the feelings and pains of another is fine and holy.

And yet, there is even more than charity to married love. Nobody would want simply to be the object of another's charity. It suggests the dole too much. So the next step higher:

Philia.

This Greek root appears in words like *Philadelphia* and *philanthropy.* Literally, it is "love of man." *Philia* is comrade-type liking for one another.

The idea of compatibility is suggested. You see eye to eye with the other one. You both enjoy the same things. You get along. You might even both *dislike* similarly. You vibrate together.

It is highly probable that most marriages are consummated on this level! "We are really comfortable with each other," I have heard many newlyweds say.

The trouble with this kind of love—*philia*—is that the years do different things to us. Whereas couples may be perfectly mated at age twenty, they may develop incompatibility by forty. Health, finances, children, living conditions, in-laws, emotional changes may affect husband and wife differently. Some wag described *incompatible* as the condition when the husband no longer has *income*, and the wife is no longer *patible!*

Agape.

The first four loves are to be seen as human, generated and measured by the Adam side of us. They have their places, but lack the power of *agape*. The reason is *religious*.

Agape comes from the New Testament and refers to perfect love (John 3:16; I Corinthians 13), which comes from a perfect God. It also has infinite or perfect characteristics in that it "does not fail"; "bears all things, believes all things, hopes all things, endures all things."

Of course, such love is absolute, and we are full of faults. We will never *achieve* it, but this does not mean we cannot *receive* it. We become channels of it, not sources; we are canals through which it flows to others. We reach for it in worship; we pass it to others in terms of kindness, patience, understanding, and forgiveness.

The key to such a love is "unmerited favor." This love is given not for what we get out of it (as with *epithamia*), but because God, our source, is love.

Therefore *agape* is godly loving, given in God's name. It doesn't depend upon what other people *are*, but on what we believe.

~~~ 3—ABSTINENCE OR TEMPERANCE ABOUT LIQUOR ~~~

The safest automobile driver will be sober,
 know the rules of the road,
  have his car in good repair,
   fasten his seat belt,
    drive defensively.
Some who follow these pointers may still have wrecks, but not so often.

The law of averages works that way with marriage.

Many who drink socially and privately will have no problem. And some non-drinkers can have smashups.

There are thousands who will celebrate their golden wedding anniversaries who have had social drinks for years.

Yet in my records, among those who have ended marriage, eight out of ten have not been helped by their cups.

Statistically, success in marriage corresponds to the amount of alcohol used. The home in gravest danger is intemperate. Next come temperate people. But the winner and still champion is the family where alcoholic beverages are not on the shopping list!

In more than thirty years of marriage counseling, I have

yet to find a marriage helped or saved by drinking. Marriage may fail through the years for many reasons,

but with liquor, it's quicker.

～• 4—WISDOM IN HANDLING MONEY •～

Married people need sense with dollars! This is because faults in finances have voided many an otherwise faultless home.

It's a shame that people who mean so much to one another can be separated by money. How much they have, or how little, is not the factor; it's how they view it. And the wrong attitude toward money may be at either extreme:

> when it means nothing,
> when it means everything.

Let's visit a couple of homes, for examples:

This family is writhing in debt.

✪ Tad works all day in a factory.

  ✪ He moonlights every evening and weekends, to bring home the cash.

    ✪ There are four children.

      ✪ His wife, June, sometimes hires a sitter, so she can also help financially.

Besides their monthly house and car payments, this family is more than $5,000 behind. With a universal credit card, June bought clothes, groceries, appliances, and gadgets far above income and real needs. Nearly all of what $5,000 bought has been eaten, broken, or worn out. So they are paying for a dead horse. June is a compulsive spender, but Tad hasn't managed wisely, either.

"What is money, compared to the things we want or need?" he asked. That *is* a great question: what *is* money?

The answer is that money can be *whatever you make it.* Granted, a number of surprise demands may carry you off track—you determine money's status. If it's *nothing,* you have bought a lie. It becomes your master.

So Tad and June will either adopt more sensible attitudes or suffer. Their home of joy awaits the day of finer judgment.

With Claud and Bess, the story was the opposite.

   ✪ Claud was a financial Scrooge.

      ✪ For him, money ruled all.

         ✪ He made a good salary, and managed every dime of it himself.

            ✪ The family walked the chalkline as he drew it.

Financially, this family was in top shape. First there were modest savings in the Building and Loan. Next came properties, then bonds and stocks. Claud took the latest papers on the Stock Market and finance.

But the human part smelled; they were money slaves. Other items, like good times, relaxation, jolly conversation, and entertainment of friends, were de-valued. Claud's family was well-dressed, neat, opulent, clean, reverent, courteous—everything but cheerful!

The result was that Bess began seeking something money couldn't buy.

That was consideration and human kindness.

It came with a fellow from high-school days who moved

to town. The first casual conversations grew to interest, then friendship and involvement.

Claud learned too late. Today he watches over his fortune, emptyhearted.

So money can mean *nothing* or *everything*. In either case, it plays havoc for keeps.

The most workable methods include these steps:

1. Give something.
   2. Save something.
      3. Have a "gentleman's agreement" about how the periodic check will be spent.
         4. Watch personal expenditures that may fault other family needs.
            5. Spend sensibly . . . obtain counsel if needed.
               6. Enjoy the rest with thanksgiving and abandon!

————◆●◆————

So marriages based upon a good experience of religion, maturity, temperance, and finances are safest.

————◆●◆————

But what happens when marriage is on the rocks? Divorce, the cancellation of the arrangements, is a rampant fact.

We cannot improve the record by condemnation.

Sometimes it's the only way out, actually to be recommended. Even deeply conservative people have had to "see the judge."

If it's a contested situation, then, of course, dig in for the duration. A feud may go on for years. Children are caught in the maelstrom of alienation from one parent or another.

In one case, both parents remarried, and neither step-parent would accept the daughter. She ran away from both homes at fourteen, and was picked up, living common-law with a man in his forties.

If the separation agreement is peaceful and cooperative, divorce brings less pain. Without being cavalier about it, many couples have "agreed to disagree," and gone their separate ways.

———————◆•❖•◆———————

Some *avant-garde* counselors recommend "term marriages."

Then couples would set a possible terminus date, instead of marrying "till death us do part."

This could bring more problems than it erases. Children, for instance, would wonder about whether the "contract" would be renewed. There's enough of this kind of anxiety already.

"Orderly marriage" is also being disrupted by communal arrangements. Here children appear by what is claimed to be pure, loving relationships; and adults, sans license, sans ceremony, claim their married life to be ideal —time will tell.

Add to these developments the erosion of family clusters, and there is just cause for concern.

And alarm.

One tragic element is at the base of the problem: *the absence of instruction about marriage in our high schools.*

If a girl plans on doing office work, she studies typing,

bookkeeping, English, and business machines. Then she may work from two to four years.

But one day, here comes the bride! Now she may enter for as many as forty or fifty years the "occupation" of being a homemaker and wife, for which she has had no specific training.

Perhaps she has taken some cooking and sewing. And maybe Common Learnings have given small reference to the total picture.

But she will not learn about the factors favorable or damaging to marriage.

She will not know the probabilities of one attitude succeeding over another.

She (or her spouse) will enter marriage, *playing it by ear.*

"For better or for worse" is a realistic phrase that can be spelled out in case studies. But they will not know of the possibilities. Family planning, sex education, homemaking, the use of money, the sensitivity-training to understand feelings, are lacking.

It is no wonder that so many marriages are doomed.

———————

Meanwhile, back home! If divorce seems the only way out, let it be done as decently, as considerately, as quietly, as reverently as possible.

Some lawyers are more devoted to conciliatory directions than others. Avoid opportunist attorneys.

Seek pastoral advice.

Be discreet and kindly.

Try to redeem the bad times by the best spirit.

And may the good Lord take you kindly through!

If, on the other hand, your marriage sings from one day to another, celebrate!

God has made it His gift. Receive it with humility and thanksgiving.

And perhaps you may inspire your kind of success in your children, your friends, and neighbors.

Married life was meant to be beautiful.

If it is, hold that treasure in precious trust.

12
In-laws Who Have It Made

You may be among the lucky people who enjoy your relatives by law.

If you are, thank the Lord and pass this chapter on to someone else.

Unfortunately for many, it's a drag to put up with these non-blood family people. They need to study the in-laws who have it made.

Two purposes are served by this:

It helps them understand their in-laws;

It encourages them to *be* better in-laws.

Generally, in-laws go second-class. They are aliens, stemming from another family tree.

Marriage has given them a status as adopted members of the clan. They are related, but not by blood.

And if an in-law has excesses—too old, too fat, too ugly or pushy—write *trouble* larger, unless all this is balanced by grace. In many cases, absence will make hearts grow fonder.

The mother-in-law takes the unkindest cuts. Sometimes it amounts only to good-natured ribbing. But not always.

Many husbands and wives actually visualize their mothers-in-law to be like this caricature: she has a raspy voice, sixty extra pounds, a huge open mouth and loose dentures, and charges in like four five-star generals marching abreast.

Legendary?

We wish we could keep it that way.

Every modern study reveals mothers-in-law to be the worst losers.

They suffer the most, though, because sometimes they have the closest views of all kinds of wrong. And often they have to help care for the children, provide financial assistance, and deal with the troubles of *their* in-laws.

Next to mother-in-law come the others. Sisters, brothers, and fathers are often faced with making something real from the artificial ties that bind them.

But you'd better believe that all in-laws are not so badly in Dutch. Some of them "have it made" better even than the blood relations. Their families celebrate them.

Maybe it's because they are so personable and swell, they'd get along with anybody.

Often they are respected and loved because the people they live with are that great, too.

And sometimes, there's a mutual agreement that says, "Look: you are an in-law to us, but we are in-laws to you, too. So let's learn how to be the best in-laws!"

This is the voice of experience.

For twenty-three years we had an aunt-in-law in our home. Auntie Murray was aunt-by-marriage to my wife Jean. That put her legally even farther away from me.

Auntie scored high in a delicate art—living with people who are indirectly related.

She, and thousands of other magnificents, could not be caricatured as culprits, never as outlaws.

Here's how they became, and stayed "in":

✎❀ **I** ❀✎

They did not count themselves automatically in.

This is something to be earned. No in-law should expect his legal status to be *ipso facto* a loving relationship.

The experience of becoming an adopted member of the family must lead to *acceptance.* Thus the WELCOME mat is at the door.

Don't take the following paragraph literally, but see it as a parable on how an in-law makes it:

The front door is first. If it's slammed tight by word, attitude, or suggestion, he's not going to get in. Next is the living-room. If he wins this round, he might gain access to a bedroom overnight. Later, it could be several nights. If he's needed and appreciated, he might get to the kitchen, which is where tastes often clash. By generous treatment, he might even be welcome to open the refrigerator. And finally, should he need the place, and be offered it, he could find all doors open, completely at home.

But pin this at the top of the board: Successful in-laws take nothing for granted. Approval and favor are earned degrees.

✎❀ **II** ❀✎

They didn't move in, no matter what.

Many a young matron has said, following her father's

death, "Now mother, you must come live with us. We want you."

She may have been completely sincere. Or it might have been filial duty.

Sometimes, of course, it's the only human and rational thing to do. If the in-law is old, poor, or helpless, be "family," and make room. Do it graciously, even when it isn't convenient.

You might even find the boarding in-law an asset.

But no matter how hospitable the invitation, it should be accepted only after checking all angles.

Maybe another home?

How about the living arrangements? Finances? Personalities?

Finally, if living together *is* the answer, make it good!

✔️ III 👁️

They held their tongues.

Most boarding in-laws are *older* than the relatives they live with. This means they have lots of valuable experience. *Anybody* ought to sit quietly and scoop up all this wisdom.

Not with the really "in"-laws!

They often have sore tongues from biting them.

They may make excuses of needing to go to the bathroom, or have a fake coughing fit, so they may exit gracefully.

Later, if a Family member *asks* them for advice or a discussion, great. They're in. They're accepted.

But in-laws ask for trouble, if, on the spot,

97

    ✪ while words are flying,

      ✪ an issue is boiling,

        ✪ a decision is to be made, or

          ✪ there's a piece of bad judgment being shown, they dig in, hold their ground, and put in their wisdom.

Repeat this three times: In-laws who have it made didn't get there by talking their way in!

✺ IV ✺

They were not always present.

Living with non-blood people can be a lonely existence. It gets worse if circumstances are unpleasant.

So the skillful in-laws know when to "blow." *Examples:*

One mother-in-law we know manages to visit another relative or friends at least one full day a week.

This one's a grandmother. When her family is having a visitor, she doesn't sit in on every conversation. The discussion does not need to include her.

An aunt seldom eats breakfast with her family, or she'll go out for lunch or dinner now and then.

A father-in-law takes trips or goes fishing, so he'll be away several days a month. It gives the family a break.

Even an invalid mother-in-law provides for someone else to come care for her several days a month.

The point: Be as pleasant as you can. Consider yourself lucky if you have it made with your in-laws.

But don't assume you're so wonderful the Family can't pass an hour or a day without you.

◈ V ◈

They realized they were guests.

Sure. They'd rather be known as *people* and be accepted. That comes if it's not insisted upon.

But a guest is a guest—not a proprietor, not a counselor, advisor, commentator, or queen or patriarch.

Their manners, these grand operators, are those of "company." Of course, it's hard to be *company* over many years, but the keen in-law realizes he is there by the courtesy and invitation of his hosts.

It's their house, not his.

◈ VI ◈

They avoided power tactics.

One of the worst of these is to use *money* as a lever. Host in-laws should be most cautious in accepting any financial or material assistance. Too often, it carries the reminder, "Don't forget what I've done for you; be good to me."

Other power media are:

Age—"Don't forget it; I've lived longer than you."

Name—"The Jones family, *my* family, is one of the finest in Jonesville."

Education—"Now Jersild, the famous authority on adolescent psychology, writes . . ."

Emotion—Before I lost my dear husband, I promised him that I would always . . ."

Prejudice—"I always wondered how it would be to live with a family where so little time is spent in reading . . ."

Game-playing—"Poor, weak, little I—nobody feels sorry for me. I guess I'll just have to give up. . . ."

Religion—"Now the *Bible* says . . ."

These sick games have raised blisters in many families.

They are the misuse of Power.

They must be replaced by the cleaner force of sincere love.

✺ VII ✺

They offered, but did not force, their assistance.

It's a shame that older people can't always soft-pedal their wisdom. Experience has lined the walls of memory with examples—what works, what fails.

Only the careful survive giving advice; only the appreciated succeed in helping.

Better by far to know what an in-law wants you to do or say, before stepping in.

✺ VIII ✺

They checked on things once in awhile.

On the surface, life might seem cool and smooth. Our favorite in-laws do not take this for granted.

They call the family in, or speak one by one to persons, and ask, "How am I doing?" This can start a good dialogue. Get down to brass tacks.

And maybe the host in-laws will even take stock of *themselves* and do some changing.

There's no guarantee that a thing can be so good it will never need improving.

100

55071

✧ IX ✧

They were short on self-pity.

(Of course, it helps if the host in-laws are high on charity and understanding.)

But superior people always fight the plague of feeling sorry for themselves.

How they do it I don't know. Maybe it's religious faith. Maybe it's rugged determination. Maybe it's being benign and humble.

It's more likely to amount to being mature and whole.

Going from middle to old age is a time to evaluate the past. Sometimes it's a depressing experience.

Being bored and unhappy with the present can cause even more difficulty.

Becoming discouraged about an empty future caps the climax.

In-laws who are in trouble in any or all of these departments, should tell it to their preacher or priest and get lots of help.

✧ X ✧

They looked toward the future, not the past.

"Now when I was a little girl," can turn off anybody, if heard over much. But that's not the point. The person who talks this way continually hasn't entered the present generation. He's not interested in the contemporary. The good days are always "back when." Tomorrow is the day he'd just as soon not live to see.

Aged in-laws have been truly loved and honored when they have decided to keep a growing interest in what their

101

host in-laws are doing. They offer encouragement and praise for achievement.

ᴥᴥ XI ᴥᴥ

They did nice things.

I want to tell you about Nellie. Nellie was born with an ugly red-and-blue birthmark that started to the left of her left eye. It covered the side of her face and disappeared down her neckline. She was the sister of Harvey. She lived with Harvey, his wife, and nine children. Besides taking care of many of the chores, she vicariously enjoyed the fun of the large family. She kept a record of every birthday, graduation, marriage, death—and she sent cards, wrote notes, became the family recorder and authority.

Over many years, Nellie was a jewel to her folks.

ᴥᴥ XII ᴥᴥ

They didn't fight.

To edit a famous cigarrette advertisement, "They'd rather switch than fight." In some way, most in-laws can find another arrangement. If life with other in-laws hasn't been favorable, every effort should be made to reconcile. If that fails, a move should be explored.

But if relocation is impossible, the in-law must learn to go second-class. In no case does he insist on his way. He never risks disturbing the peace.

Often this is next to impossible, because of the badgering of the host in-laws.

It's a time for truest sympathy.

Rules, rules, rules!

You and I don't like them. They seem rigid, indigestible, loathsome.

All laws and regulations depend upon the "citizen." He won't follow them unless he has

ACCEPTANCE

AND

MOTIVATION.

What could make these suggestions for in-laws palatable to you?

It is the person between.

For instance, say your assignment is a working arrangement with your wife's brother. Maybe your "programmer" tells you it won't work. Maybe you'd rather be out of it.

But your wife, who loves you, also loves her brother. Do your best for her sake.

She is the one between.

Either she can be ground to bits by two people she needs, or she can be surrounded by understanding and support.

FINAL REMINDER AND CHECKPOINT: You *have* an in-law; you *are* an in-law.

Adjust!

13
Recipes for Getting Along

Abstract principles and suggestions have a way of evaporating.

So let's see how some warm bodies have starred in family peace.

≈≈≈≈ 1—APPRECIATION PLACE ≈≈≈≈

A Kansas farmer had just completed another "round" of cutting hay. It was 100° in the shade, and he was under a blistering sun.

The water jug—you know, the kind covered with burlap, kept wet to cool the water—was empty.

So he called to his son.

"Ned, please bring me a drink from the well."

Hanging on the pump was a white porcelain cup, "community property."

Ten-year-old Ned filled it and brought it over, not noticing that his forefinger lopped over the edge.

So he didn't see the brown stream of dirt that wriggled down into the water.

Dad noticed it, but drank without reference to the mud. Then he said, "Thanks, Ned. I never had a better drink."

Of course, he *could* have hammered Ned down. Dirt is dirt. Carelessness is bad *Karma*.

But this kindly farmer chose what was important. He had his drink, and Ned had fetched it for him. He honored the act.

Small incident, big person.

Forgiveness in overalls, grace dripping with sweat.

⚬⚬⚬· 2—"HE'S MY BROTHER" ·⚬⚬⚬

Clem B. was our town's favorite undertaker.

You could say this in spite of the fact that he was the only one. He had an understanding spirit which made folks trust and respect him.

One day we were driving back from a funeral. He told me about his brother in Iowa.

Five years earlier, Clem had staked him $8,000 to go into retail furniture.

But things went from bad to worse. His unshaven brother often came to work with a hangover, and opened late. Accounts payable were neglected; collections on installments were long overdue. Several trips by Clem produced no improvement in his brother's actions.

Finally the store closed, and Clem lost more than $12,000.

I responded, "So that ended your relations with him?"

Clem looked surprised, then calmly capped it: "Why, of course not! He's still my brother!"

⚬⚬⚬· 3—THE HORSE BEFORE THE CART ·⚬⚬⚬

Anne was in my study planning her wedding.

Hardly any weddings "come from the books" any more; no two are alike.

She made an unusual request. When the vows were to be repeated, she wanted these lines added:

> . . . and I forgive you in advance for whatever you may do to offend me.

Usually forgiveness is kept on a shelf until somebody trespasses. Then you consider whether to reach for it and use it.

The transaction should run: The offender offends; the offended calls the foul; the sinner asks for pardon; forgiveness is granted, followed by restitution and/or reconciliation.

But Anne had a superior idea. Forgiveness was built into her marriage from "here comes the bride." She preferred to be carried over the threshold with a will to be tolerant, for better and for worse.

ᔆᔆ· 4—COOL HAND LUKE ·ᔆᔆ

Luke wasn't his name, but we'll call him that. And he wasn't known for playing it cool. He had a humped nose, the result of a fight in his teens. He was made of *bang, whop, biff,* and *wow!*

But he got that name in earlier years.

One evening he came home from his switchman chores on the railroad. As usual, he showered and put on something light for supper. Then he opened the mail.

One letter was from his son, aged twenty, who lived in Cleveland. We'll call him Buck. He had been away a year, following two semesters of college in which he made the dean's dishonor roll.

So he decided to pull the Prodigal, and go where nobody could be checking on him.

You'd have to know, too, that during high school he had been no bargain to live with.

How does a man like Luke deal with a boy like Buck? A string of traffic tickets, wrecked cars, bad report cards, days of goofing off . . .

Dads of kids like Buck lose a lot of sleep.

The letter was like a garbage list. It went something like this:

> You never understood me. You were so full of great big schemes for my future, you had no time for my feelings. You lost whatever temper you had when I was around. I know I did wrong, but I don't know whether it was heredity or environment. Mom dug me sometimes, but she was so prim and perfect. I felt like a villain whenever I was around her. But you—I guess I could only say that the reason I am the way I am, is that you are what you are. Forgive me for saying it, but this kid could have had a better father . . .

Luke read the letter, and for a brief, violent moment, he flared. "I'll write that damn scamp a letter so hot it'll take asbestos paper. Who does he think he is?"

He crumpled and uncrumpled the letter three times.

But just as he was reaching for a tablet, he stopped short. As he had learned to do, he went down in the basement and dawdled at his bench.

It was good therapy.

He never acknowledged the letter. One month passed. Three. Six. Nine. A year.

Many times he resisted the temptation to write.

Then one Sunday night at nine the telephone rang. It was Buck.

"Dad? How are you? Oh, I'm OK, I guess. Working at a Texaco station, saving a little. Going steady with a girl named May. Yeah, she's real nice. Dad . . . I wrote you a letter about a year ago, and I don't know if you got it, but it was kinda bad. I really didn't mean it—all of it —but I had some things to get off my chest. I hope you will try to forget it, and won't hold it against me. I'm sorry."

Luke was, for the first time in years, speechless. He tried to clear his throat.

What he said in return isn't important here.

He had won the ball game. Errors he had made. But the score was coming out right.

5—WHO MAKES YOUR BED FOR YOU?

And this story is for those who haven't caught it: A family is made up of people who share the work load.

You can whip somebody into work; you can offer money. You may try scolding, reasoning, ordering, crying, insulting, jesting. But *desire* is the invisible, chromosomal motivation that sparks action.

This is a love story:

The Ferrell twins are professionally outstanding today. One is a dentist, the other a college professor. They were two of six children. In college days their mother took in washing to help pay the bills, and their father moonlighted in janitorial work.

Everyone in the family had some kind of job.

The boys carried papers.

One evening they came in from delivering the route and noticed Mother Ferrell etched in weariness. She might become ill. They spoke to the others.

At the close of dinner they announced that for the next month the kids would cook dinner and wash all dishes.

"But what would I do?" asked the mother who considered cooking her special duty. "Now I'm all right. Don't worry about me."

The family held firm.

At first Mrs. Ferrell seemed lost. But after an evening or two, she was able to relax in the porch swing. She had time to trim her roses, or drop in to chat with a neighbor. Gradually her shoulders straightened a little, and her eyes were clearer.

In a month she was eager to get back to evening meals. She was so much better.

But nothing physically could be compared to the way she felt inside. That's the way it is with a family of helpers.

6—I WOULD BE TRUE, FOR THERE ARE THOSE WHO TRUST ME

Only people over forty may know these lines. They come from an old Sunday school song.

Bob and Cecile had been married only a year.

He traveled for a clothing company. Cecile was lonely, because Bob would leave Monday mornings and return Friday evenings.

Sometimes during these lonely days, she asked herself: "Now what does Bob do on those evenings out in the territory? How can I be sure? I've known men as good as he who have stepped out on their wives. And besides, he may be real careful for years, and then one night—"

So one weekend, she spilled her concerns to Bob. She was embarrassed. It sounded as though she didn't trust him.

She took a dangerous risk, because a marriage of only a year could be nixed.

But Bob ranked hero. He said, "Tell you what: I'll let you know exactly where I'll be every week—the towns, the motels—and you are welcome to call me any night or even come and drop in on me. How's that?"

Fair enough.

That satisfied Cecile.

She probably wouldn't do it.

But in about two months, she did! She boarded a bus and rode 150 miles, arriving around six—and went to the motel. Bob had registered, but he was out, probably to dinner.

So she waited.

And waited.

And waited.

At 11:30, still no Bob. Cecile felt green, blue, red, yellow—all at once.

At 11:45 Bob strolled in. He and another salesman had been to a movie. Bob took her to meet him, and the story was confirmed.

Of course, this tale *could* have ended a dozen different

ways, all tragic. That's the way it is with stories and life. Often there is only one good ending, but there could be many bad ones.

Bob and Cecile talked a couple of hours. She had a little jealous, suspicious streak erased, and Bob showed his savvy of accepting reality.

That was about twenty-two years ago. Bob still travels; Cecile still trusts him.

Here is one of the best marriages, because faith was confirmed and accepted.

Let us not let any lack of trust destroy our best energies.

⮜ 7—AND FINALLY . . . ⮞

This will take a couple of stories.

You are exceptional if you don't mind talking about the end of the trail. You have more company if you'd rather not. You might be all alone if you enjoy it.

You *know* it's there, this final wrap-up. Sweep it under the rug. Pretend things go on and on endlessly. But one day you'll find something like a *finis,* and that will be that.

The last of enjoying good health.

—Or of a period when you have lived with others.

—Or graduation.

—Or marriage.

—Or divorce.

—A crippling accident.

And, well—death.

There are two ways to view these final decrees:

One is to face the finish amazed, and looking back over

what has been. Sometimes this is with regrets, but it *can* be beautiful, too, if you've had it good.

But the other is to live in the *now*, with some consciousness that there will be a closing day and hour.

Religious people have a name for this in ethics. It is called *teleology*, which is the science of final events or values. To telephone is to speak to the other end of the line. Telegraph is writing it one place and having it read another. The *here* and *now* are vitally connected with the *there* and *later*.

Robert Louis Stevenson put it fatally:

Sooner or later, we all sit down to the banquet of consequences.

The first illustration is about Sue.

You would like Sue, but not this tear-jerk story.

Her mother died at forty-six. She had been beautiful and well, or so everybody thought.

She and Sue had, as Sue put it, "bitched back and forth for years."

This particular morning Sue, aged sixteen, had left for school after hurling a final insult at her mother. That afternoon at bridge, Sue's mom keeled over with a cerebral hemorrhage, and that was it.

Skip this page if you are tenderhearted. Stomp on the book.

Standing in the hall of their home, Sue said, "If I could only have five minutes—two minutes—five seconds—to tell her that I'm sorry—that I have always loved her!"

———— •♦•————

The second instance you could apply to the need for

people of all ages to become *Adult*. This is so important, because the *Child* is known to live only for today.

Hang the Red Cross talk about driving defensively: Rod was an *offensive* driver. He badgered his Cutlass through town as though it were indestructible, the streets were all his, and other drivers were to be conquered.

One evening, he and Rene were on their way to a rock festival in the country. They were on the committee, and needed to be there early. But they were late. Rod was at least fifteen miles over every speed zone limit. His glass belt tires were put to their worst test. Every start and stop left a pair of black ribbons.

At the edge of town, he said, "Come on, Baby, show 'em what you've got!" the speedometer needle traced the speed within the first mile to 105. Rene, sitting close, began to tense.

"Whatsa matter, Honey? Gettin' chicken or sump'n'?" he asked.

Rene was quiet for a few more moments, then went into action. She pretended to be ill, and slumped down and away from Rod. He pulled quickly over to the side.

Then she took the keys from the ignition and sat up.

"Rod, I love you, and I like almost everything about you. But I've got to get you to see something real important. Do you know there are at least ten people riding with us today? There are our folks. If we were in a wreck and had to be hospitalized for months, it would take all their money. This is happening every day, Rod. And my brothers and your sisters are here too, because they would be affected by any tragedy we would have. And besides, I'm wearing your ring, and we are planning on getting

113

married. We hope to have at least two children. They are riding with us today too."

"Wow! Listen to the Reverend," said Rod. "How long did it take you to whomp up that sermon?"

"Just the last few minutes, Rod. People have accidents even when they obey speed rules. And more people have bad ones when they drive the way you've been. Let's take it easy, shall we? After all, there's more to think about than today's rock festival. OK?"

Naturally, Rod was stabbed in his pride and had a few bad moments. But the rest of the way he cooled it.

Rene added the dimension of the *future* to the *now*.

These instances have covered the following principles for getting along:

1. Bigness, grace, magnanimity.
2. Remembering our blood relationships.
3. Forgiveness a principle, leading to forgiveness the act.
4. Cool understanding.
5. Sharing the work load, part of Adulthood.
6. Trust offered, trust accepted.
7. Seeing what is down the track.

Do not settle for these pointers as only "good rules." They serve as supports for family hope.

14
The Seven Parts of Kindness

Your dream family won't spring from nothing.

To use computer talk, it is "programmed."

Whatever is fed in as schedules and hours, comes out as tangibles. Your specific decisions and "data" put flesh on the bones.

Principles become policies; attitudes set the stage for actions.

Take kindness, for an important example. No family survives without it.

Yet it isn't enough just to "be kind." You need to give internal and external attention to the details.

Begin with the general condition that *kindness* is the method observed by *kin*. Both words come from one Anglo-Saxon root. Kind people have a covenant with one another which makes them "family."

Then you follow with the ingredients. They are as essential as clay and straw for making bricks.

Kindness has seven principal parts:

---❦ PART 1—EMPATHY ❧---

Careful manners need a foundation. Actions have a way of revealing something deeper.

Human science is concerned with the world of *feelings*. It's not only what another says; it's how you feel about it, or how he does. It's not simply what you hear; it's whether you pick up some meaning, within or beyond the words.

Sensitivity training techniques revolve around this element. In fact, "sensitivity" probes into the "gutsy" responses. Persons in controlled groups learn to experience communication-in-depth. This frankness routs out hostilities, fear, angers, and makes reconciliation possible.

It should lead to personal growth.

But everybody will not be able to take sensitivity training. Only those who are able to accept the evaluation that is bound to come should consider it. Hypersensitive people prosper in less radical therapy.

The family can actually provide a continuous setting for personal growth. It is done through *empathy*.

This is the process of projecting yourself into the feelings and concerns of others.

It is the opposite of self-aggrandizement.

The Chamber of Mirrors in the palace at Versailles, France, provides a unique experience. As you walk around, you are poignantly aware of yourself. Everywhere you look is another *you*.

The self-centered individual tries to live in his own chamber of mirrors. He sees only himself. The world seems to be all his. You might feel that such a person is a rare criminal. To be entirely selfish would take an evil genius.

But the element of self-service is in everyone. Even

"enlightened self-interest" is still self-interest. It can too easily be perverted to malicious self-interest.

When King Louis IV of France saw Gobelin tapestry for the first time, he issued an order forbidding anyone else the right to possess it.

And in Agra, India, stands the breathtaking Taj Mahal. The Emperor Shah Jahan used 22,000 slaves and took 22 years to build it. The designer and superintendent was an Italian. After it was finished, Jahan had the man blinded and both hands severed, so he could not build anything like it for others.

Probably this was one of the reasons why Carl Sandburg said that "exclusive" was the ugliest word in the English language.

The aim of psychology and religion is to dedicate egos to the love of God and man. Family success thrives on this.

Until the "I" is removed as the object of affection, kindness goes begging.

And empathy has no "i" in it.

⸺⸰❦ PART 2—CHARITY ⸙⸰⸺

Here's an overworked word.

To appreciate *charity,* you will need to see it in a new light. "Charity" too often suggests a kind of dole—a handout of something to make you feel good.

Actually it has an inspired suggestion.

You begin with the logical approach that if you will be kind to anyone, you must appreciate him first. You treat him honorably, but not because something will come back to you. You are completely grateful for *him.*

And being kind is one of the best ways to tell him so.

It's all wrapped up in the word charity, itself. Coming from the Latin *caritas*, it suggests a kind of grace or loving-kindness.

But this root grows up into the French word *cher*, meaning "dear"—related to our "cherish." So the one you cherish is important—to you. You treat him like a prized friend. You love, need, value, and respect him. This means you will not want him hurt in any way. Nor will you miss the chance to encourage him.

"Pop" Rhodes raised horses at the Nebraska University Extension farm at North Platte. After the magnificent Percherons were no longer needed for draft purposes, he began to raise Morgans. One day, he took me to the corral, and when he whistled, two colts trotted up to him. He gave them gentle pats and soft words.

Then he explained: "These animals are very sensitive. If I would just once give a harsh tone or gesture, it would take me days to overcome it. They come to me, because they know they have a friend."

This kind of experience judges and inspires us at the same time. We begin to remember all the times we forgot to be kind, and how hard it was to rebuild.

But maybe we could also be inspired to try harder today and tomorrow. Kindness is based on charity—appreciating the priceless in other people.

PART 3—PATIENCE

At this point you learn that kindness is not always fun. That's because its nature is such that normal, "human" responses aren't necessarily peaceful.

Patience is a beautiful quality when others see it in action. But to the one who uses it, there is inside agony. The word derives from the Latin *pati,* meaning "to suffer."

Of course, most adults feel that there are times to blow the whistle and call fouls. Dr. Jesse Baird, long-time president of San Francisco Theological Seminary, was preaching in his home church. His wife and four sons sat in the third row. During the sermon the boys began to pass notes and visit.

Dr. Baird took it for awhile. But finally he stopped in the middle of a paragraph and shouted, "BOYS!"

That did it.

And *it* was called for!

In most family situations there is tension between being polite and taking practicable measures. To this, you add such concerns as

being on time,

meeting obligations with the library,

considering the neighbors,

making it to church,

sending thank-you notes.

Inner knots multiply. They extend to produce hot words, angry frowns, hasty remarks.

At such a moment to act kindly may seem hypocritical.

You want to be honest and tell the other person how it galls you.

Most counselors agree that it is wrong *not* to report your grievances; let the laggard know how you feel! But this must be done sparingly. And it must not reflect your selfishness. Honest concern and friendly respect should temper what you say.

The most likely pitfalls in forgetting to be patient are these:

a. *Not having stored up good ideas in the first place.* The ancient Chinese proverb is "Patience and a mulberry leaf will make a silken gown." You must be thinking about the total idea—have it in mind.

b. *Preoccupation.* This means to have your own priorities so indelible, you have little room to consider those of others. They interrupt you. The result is a flash of resentment.

c. *Reacting before you have all the facts in.* Many a fine point is lost when you've misjudged or prejudged a family member. Rebuilding takes a long time.

Your physical condition will sometimes trick you into impatient reactions. Maybe the worries of the job or finances, or whatever, could nudge you off guard. There are all kinds of situations ready to scuttle your best attempts.

But to grow, head these conditions off with the ONE need: *determination to be patient.*

And that takes suffering.

--◦◄{ PART 4 — GENTILITY }►◦--

The close of the 1970s will record sick days for gentle words and methods.

Revolutionary elements have attacked the practice of manners. Obscene words spatter every kind of medium.

Direct reference to persons, name-calling, and vulgar references have become common.

We have been exposed to the dirty fingernails of speech.

We get to look like what we look at. Television and movie offerings have capitalized on violence in voice, reaction, and pastime.

One winter I was home for four days with laryngitis. Just to study what was going on, I listened daily to soap operas. It made me sicker!

And I soon understood how suggestive the scenes were! Teen-agers would learn to corner their parents with illogical cruelty. Husbands or wives might take up suggestions on how to be sarcastic. Seldom was a comment taken for what it was meant to say. If words were weapons, the TV would have been flowing with blood.

Here are two definitions of a gentleman:

The first is by John Galsworthy. "The essential characteristic of a gentleman: The will to put himself in the place of others; the horror of forcing others into positions from which he would himself recoil; the power to do what seems to him to be right, without considering what others may say or think."

The second comes from Charles Wiggins. "A gentleman is a man who is clean inside and who never looks up to the rich or down to the poor; who can lose without whimpering; who can win without bragging; who is considerate to all women, children, and old people—or those who are weaker than he is. A man who is too brave to lie; too generous to cheat; whose pride will not let him loaf, and who insists on doing his share of work in any capacity; a man who thinks of his neighbor before he thinks of himself, and asks only to share equally with all men the blessings which God has showered upon us."

It should be admitted that there are some situations that call out violent reactions. A sense of justice would have it no other way. But generally, *the family* will be built upon kindness, and kindness is based on the foundation of politeness.

By this you show common respect and courtesy.

There are no substitutes.

—◄ PART 5 — TONE ►—

Even the most loving feelings will not come through a harsh disposition.

Generally we think of the voice, and that is important. But there is a personality tone that includes looks, motions, attitudes, and reactions (see Chapter Two).

Kindness is a generator, sending impulses to every part of personality. All the actions together spell *tone*—the total vibration of *the real you*.

Meet Tammy, our eight-year-old wire-haired terrier. I'll call her to my side, and say, "Tammy, you are a stupid little mongrel, a dirty dog, not worth the food we buy for you every month. Dogs like you come a dime a dozen. You're ready for the glue factory."

When I say this, she licks my hand and stays around for more.

You know the reason: it's the tone of voice. These cruel words are said with tenderness. This is what Tammy hears.

The boy who became the famous movie magnate Louis B. Mayer, came home one afternoon full of hate. A school chum had just beaten him up.

His mother had heard him say, "Damn you!" to the boy.

She took him to the window looking out over one of the beautiful valleys of New Brunswick, Canada. There were tall hills on either side, perfect for echoes.

His mother said, "Now, Louis, say what I heard you say."

It took him a little while to get the courage, but he finally said it. "Louder," his mother urged. "Louder still!" Finally he shouted loudly enough for the echo to come back, "Damn you!"

"Now," said his mother, "try it another way. Say 'Bless you!' instead." He consented, and soon he was hearing his echo, "Bless you! Bless you!"

The tone you give will usually be the tone you get. Pleasant voices, passed back and forth across the family canyon, will fill the valleys with peace.

—⋈{ PART 6 — COOPERATION }⋈—

On December 17, 1967, Professor Christiaan Barnard, M.D., stood at the foot of a bed in a South African hospital. He spoke to Dr. Philip Blaiberg, a dental surgeon who had a permanently damaged heart, about the possibility of a heart-transplant operation, saying that he was prepared to perform one. Dr. Blaiberg responded eagerly, and promised his full cooperation.

Blaiberg was moved to a private room in the cardiac section. There he waited until January 1, 1968, when Clive Haupt, a twenty-four-year-old Negro, suffered a cerebral hemorrhage. His doctor, Basil Sacks, called the hospital where Dr. Blaiberg waited and said that he might have a donor.

Later, Haupt's wife was told her husband couldn't live. Would she allow her husband's heart to be transplanted?

Note her cooperation in replying that if someone else's life could be saved that way, she was willing.

Mrs. Haupt walked over to Clive's mother, and asked if she agreed. Again, the reply was yes.

Then a vast team went to work. The immunologists, technicians, anesthesiologists, druggists, cardiologists—experts from many medical fields—surrounded Professor Barnard. Here everybody was doing his best; every person dedicated to the team and its project.

After he recovered, Dr. Blaiberg wrote, "For me it had come to mean so much in care and devotion, kindliness and self-sacrifice by so many. . . . 'Eileen,' I said, 'the world is marvelous, just bloody marvelous!' " [1]

C. S. Lewis once said, "No clever arrangements of bad eggs ever made a good omelette." So a family is only a collection of miscellaneous protoplasm, until you have *cooperation*.

In brief, the cooperator says, "What you are doing may, or may not, be important; but since you are doing it, and I care about you, I will help you. I will not stand in your way. I will try to understand what you are doing. I can be counted upon to do my part, wherever it is for the total good."

--◄€{ PART 7 — PUNCTUALITY }€►--

Anne sat watching television. Her date saw her at

[1] Philip Blaiberg, "To the Last Heartbeat," in *Reader's Digest,* Oct., 1966, pp. 274-306, condensed from *Looking at My Heart* (New York: Stein & Day, 1969) .

Sandy's two evenings before. "I'll pick you up at about 7:30," he said.

So she had helped her mother with housecleaning all day. About 5:00 she showered and put her hair up in curlers. Now it was 8:15. Bert hadn't come.

Between the agreement two nights before and this hour, there had been no phone call to confirm the date. She just expected him to show up.

At 8:45, the horn sounded. She leaped to the door. It was Bert. Without explanation or apology, he took Anne to the movie.

"That's the way his parents are," Anne explained the next morning. "They never are on time for anything. They don't get after each other. And they just don't get excited about manners or time or anything like that."

Yet Anne had to admit it hurt to have Bert show up late. She was ready at the time he said he would come. If he couldn't have made it then, he should have called. Or when he finally arrived, he owed her an apology.

Whenever any member of the family is unpunctual, he is unkind. He says by his actions, "It doesn't matter to me that you are waiting and wondering. I'll be there when I can make it, and that's that."

Procrastination is one of the cruelest slights. It has the power to disrupt peace, and separate married partners; it can ruin the chances of young people for success; it has a long record of pain, strife, brutality, and sadism.

Usually, intentional delay is the method of the *Child*. This person aims to hurt. He wouldn't use any suspect weapons like clubs or brutal words. He may never record a misdemeanor you could see.

But one thing he can do is to *make people wait.*

And those affected suffer and suffer and suffer. Patience and understanding run dry; genuine concern leads to panic. That's how it is with those who wait.

But how about the procrastinator himself?

The unpunctual one deliberately cuts out a pattern that does not fit *Adult* responsibilities. A wage-earner meets deadlines. Homemakers cannot put off duties forever.

Approval is a universal human need. We forget this too often.

But the procrastinator isn't praised much, if at all.

So, sometimes he becomes stubborn and claims he doesn't need all that praise. It then becomes a vicious cycle of

DELAY — NO PRAISE — DELAY — NO PRAISE — DELAY — NO PRAISE.

Only some healing change breaks this lazy chain.

Meanwhile, each member helps by seeing kindness as basic to joyful living. And a principal part of kindness is being punctual; this means he's practically thoughtful of the other one.

Somebody is waiting for you.

Somebody depends upon you.

Stop and consider that your procrastination has the power to express anti-love.

You'll get to it?

As you serve others—as you realize your potentials— make it on time!

15
Making Shore on Broken Pieces

The word "family" produces colorful pictures, like those you see on calendars—parents about thirty-five, with three children. They are on a picnic, at home, or going to church.

Most families do not fit the concept. Even this lovely bunch will be separated someday, leaving fragments. Some of them will form new clusters.

So most homes would be incomplete, if we must define home as including father, mother, sister, and brother.

How we fragment is well known:

   Loss of husband or wife—widowhood.

    Death of one or both parents.

     One or both parents removed by desertion or divorce.

      Death of children—or a war fatality.

       Youths who run away.

        Illness that sends the afflicted to places of care.

         Separation by tragedy, as in crime or natural disaster.

If people in these family remnants stay sweet and useful, that is "making shore."

The saying comes from the travels of the Apostle Paul. Near Cyprus (Acts 27) his boat encountered a slashing storm, washed into shallow waters.

The ship struck the reefs and began to break up; 262 passengers and crew either swam to shore or held onto wreckage and cargo, "some on boards, and some on broken pieces of the ship. And so it came to pass, that they escaped all safe to land."

They made shore on broken pieces.

And so can any fractured family! Those who want to fill the gaps with purpose try approaches like these:

1. *Acceptance.* Don't read this as resignation, but as dynamic response. A church janitor was loved by all 900 members. He explained his attitude: "I just put myself into neutral, and let them push."

Disappointment doesn't need to produce disaster. Avoid self-pity; face facts; turn your victorious self on.

2. *Do What's Necessary.* This paragraph is written at 8,400 feet above sea level, near Colorado Springs. On September 17 the hills have a one-foot blanket of snow! Outside, squirrels, magpies, and mountain jays show their amazing ability to survive. They'll stay through the winter, too. But it's done by *compensation*.

Human beings are faced with choices when storms come. They, in contrast to animals, may take the course of despair, or get busy with mature responses.

So if you have remnants, you at least have *remnants!*

Use them to build the kind of happiness that is available. Set your house, finances, relationships in order—with what you need to persist.

3. *Study*. This is not to suggest *academic boredom*. It's just smart to read up on the kinds of things others have discovered under similar situations. Lectures, books, articles—visits with people who've been through the mill—use these media to become an expert on your predicament. Know where you are, what's best to believe and do.

4. *Keep Busy*. Follow this logic: if people become mentally ill, one of the techniques for recovery is occupational therapy. So why not do what's healthy before you're ready for that kind of treatment?

One of the Menninger family said that the more food-mixers in our kitchens, the more patients they would have at their clinic! He meant that there was emotional health in the hard work once required. A pioneer mother was weary to the marrow, but as she thawed the pump, scrubbed by hand, and kept the garden, she had little room for worry.

5. *Seek Company*. This is written with reservation. There are a few who make it better alone. A writer said he was plagued by friends' visits after his wife died. They thought he needed company; he wanted to get to his writing! Most of us, though, require close friends who fill the hollows.

6. *Play*. Billy Southworth once said to a service club:

"Gentlemen, swinging a bat is a great tonic, a fine exercise. It strengthens the diaphragm. Besides, you may hit the ball!"

The fringe benefits of recreation are many. Millions keep sane and sweet with crafts. It's a kind of "show and tell" that produces interest—personality dividends. You reach out for beauty.

Wallace Hartsfield, speaking to African Methodist Episcopalians, said a person must "throw himself into the arena of life and become a participant in all that is good and wholesome, rather than being only a spectator."

7. *Serve.* This is near the top of what to do.

Sarah, a cleaning woman, told her employer about a quiet widow who lived nearby. "She's mighty extravagant," she said.

"But that can't be; she gets only a small pension. She hasn't any money to speak of."

"Yes'm," Sarah agreed. "I know that, but it isn't money I mean. That woman is always doing for other people. She's wonderfully extravagant—not with money, but with herself."

Follow roads that lead away from yourself.

8. *Keep Faith.* This has four parts.

The first is to believe in yourself. Self-respect is paramount to self-reliance.

Second, keep faith with those who may have left you. A teen-age girl lost her friend by death. She often said, "Cindy was so good, I like to stop and ask what she would do if she were here." The best memorial is in what we do.

The other side: if a relative has deserted you, keep lines of love intact. Some day the wanderer may return. Believing in him is a WELCOME sign.

Third, keep faith in faith! If we believed our *beliefs* more, and doubted our *doubts,* we'd be stronger. Madame Chiang Kai-shek wrote, "I have often been asked what faith means to me. In my own life, faith is primarily the flame that illuminates any great venture."

Finally, keep faith in God. Actually, it is impossible to be a complete atheist. People always have *some* god. If it isn't the deity Christians talk about, it can be money, sex, power, self—whatever guides us is "god."

The God of Jesus is the embodiment of perfect love, strength, joy, peace, wisdom. *Why settle for less than the best?*

These eight suggestions are possible only with the attitude of persistence.

Someone asked Jacques Cousteau, deep-sea explorer, his rule for an exciting life.

He replied: *"Always to get up one more time than I have fallen."*

Others have made shore on broken pieces.

That's where the action is.

And the victory.

16
Looking Back for Meaning

When ancient Sodom was punished for its sins, Mr. and Mrs. Lot were forewarned.

The city would be struck with the fury of God, then sink down into the salt flats south of the Dead Sea.

Their escape rested upon a strange taboo: they were not to look back (Genesis 19).

But Mrs. Lot couldn't resist the temptation.

She turned around, and became a statue of salt.

It seems unfair. Her house was being destroyed. Fond memories of living there flooded her heart, *and an act of God was taking it all away!*

Could she leave without even one farewell glance?

You will be bogged down too, if you miss the real point.

That is, you shouldn't visualize Mrs. Lot suddenly crystallizing into a "pillar of salt." Rather, she hesitated, and was lost in briny quicksand. She became *salted down* forever, because her past literally swallowed her.

The lesson comes home. Something always has to be done with earlier years. They cannot be swept under the rug. Nor can they be written off as, "That's that; what has been is over and done." It may be *over,* but it is never *done.*

The past may be beneficial or destructive. It is seldom innocuous. Each family member may look back with joy or resentment.

It depends upon how we view it.

Family people will find three times when the backward glance must be taken, and very well:

THE TEENS — THE MERIDIAN YEARS — RETIREMENT

Let's take them in that order.

THE TEENS

You wouldn't think teens would have much to look back upon. They aren't that old, maybe?

But their past is loaded with potentials for satisfaction or regret. Important events begin the day of birth. The first two or three years are saturated with material to wreck or to build life to follow.

Children flower into a world dominated by adults, especially parents. Furniture is made usually for big people. Programs and activities, for all the Disneyland diversions, primarily serve them.

Grown-ups

★ own the money,

★ drive the cars,

★ plan the meals,

★ choose the clothes, the house, the friends, the church.

Every child plans what he will do about this when he grows up.

Late childhood and early adolescence, the first attempted take-overs appear.

One teen-ager reported his impatience: "I'm too old to do what children do, and too young to do what adults do."

Another said that adolescence wasn't a period at all, but a *comma*.

Parents realize that teen-age is a baffling time. It is difficult to know how one handles the daily toss of crises. Tensions spawn and flourish, between

★ freedom to be, and limitation in discipline;

  ★ individual personal development, and consciousness of community;

    ★ love of parents, and rejection of their authority;

     ★ the pull of the gang, and home teachings.

These strains are mixed in a caldron of change. Alien ideas challenge the home rules; they offer options to upstraight doctrines and morals.

The "normal" child with "normal" parents enjoys being a human animal. It's a marvelous life. Little three-months-old loves pats and "stroking." He is free to yell, throw cereal, burp in public, and dirty his pants. *The world is his oyster.*

But by the first birthday, something begins to spoil all this.

The most traumatic reversal is potty-training. Whereas he used to be free to "let go," now there's that little chair with a hole in the seat! He has to sit there without knowing what he is supposed to do, at first.

At times he just can't make it do!

Then later, he does the job off the chair!

And then there's the "don't touch" mystery.

Beautiful rattles tempt and delight in the playpen. The vase on the coffee table is just as beautiful.

But hands off!

These and other introductions into the adult world give this tot the idea that he is *not such great material.* He is in the playpen and grown-ups manage the program. So, for this period, parents control children, and that's that.

But sometime—is it three or six or nine or twelve?— *a budding adolescent logs important personal discoveries.* That he has been missing the plays is clear. He isn't quite acceptable as he is.

But now he begins to look for flaws in his parents and other adults.

Perfection is a myth and fable.

Maybe Johnnie has been told it's bad to lose his temper. Then he hears his dad explode when he hits his thumb.

Or he might have had honesty drilled into him. But he discovers his mother hiding some money from Dad.

He learns they don't always practice what they preach.

There is still another leak in the dike of parents-child comfort:

It is the discovery that some other mothers and dads are so different. If the "difference" means more "stroking" and less demanding, the adolescent steps up his campaign against his own parents. They stand for the unpleasant past, when *Parent*-bulldozes-*Child.* The adolescent swings away from them as he finds "new parents," adults who don't discipline and drive.

At this point the tables of childhood dependence can turn with a shock.

Now the adolescent is sure *he* has the right viewpoint, and his parents do not.

The past (childhood) is condemned as bad copy. He wants to write a new script.

Such reaches for independence may cause untold pain. Freakouts, copouts, and dropouts head for the roadless life. They make kindling from direction and warning signs.

Nothing works with all adolescents, but to save some we must provide a rear-view mirror that interprets childhood helpfully.

There have been days good and bad, pleasant and revolting. But making a success out of retrospect requires "programming" things *for what they are.*

The teen-ager must see his *Child* as the yearning *to be approved.* This is a dominant appetite.

If he continues to play the game of "stroke me always," he is unprepared for anything worthy of *Adult.*

At the other extreme, he should understand that early he seeks to become *Parent.* He becomes weary of being pecked down.

So even as early as age three, he expresses his "Parent feeling" by power tactics in the nursery. He kicks his toys, domineers other children, tries to hoard the pretties. It makes him feel good to be in the driver's seat.

The *Parent-Child* techniques may be used alternately. *Whatever brings instant satisfaction will be employed.*

But the responsible *Adult* still waits in the wings. Until

he is called forth, you have a boor who demands all and gives nothing.

Parent and *Child* often rampage through adolescent years like wild horses.

The teen-ager demands autonomy and approval at the same time. He wants to make up his *own* mind, but yearns for support as he does it. Disfavor is rejected, praise preferred.

However accomplished, the adolescent will score high when he becomes a sensitive adult.

Only a change in master sentiment will convert him from the *Child* or *Parent* to produce this *Adult*.

He will shed the simper and the stomp of the child. He will knock off the inordinate desire to conquer. He will go to work.

He has no time to resent "what happened to me when I was little."

He is ready to be given responsibility, and to be enjoyed.

The families that suffer from teen-age blahs will profit from these points.

People at any age should grow into "big boys" and "big girls" as soon as possible.

The earlier they do, the sooner the dove of family peace will come home to roost.

THE MERIDIAN YEARS

Whether you are the forty-five-year-old or live with one, try to see what is happening.

137

Middle age resembles adolescence.

The teen-ager is neither child nor adult; *the middle-ager isn't old, but he isn't young, either.*

In fact, he has discovered that he has lived longer than he is gonna!

He "can do as much as he ever did," but possibly doesn't.

He is entering the age of the Five B's—

bunions, bulges, bridges, bi-focals, and baldness.

Sometimes his stomach doesn't know whether to pooch out, over, or under his belt.

And when he undresses, there's more to put out on the dresser!

On the female side (although it can be co-educational) there is "change of life"—menopause. This may be over in months, or extend to years. Sometimes it has an agenda of pain, nerves, and doctoring. It may affect the body with ailments, the emotions with depression, the mind with questions, and the personality with shocks.

Usually, though, with a physician's help, many of these symptoms may be allayed.

Experts tell us that much more is happening subconsciously. What could be the "prime of life" clouds over with

★ vocational disappointments or failures,

★ growing incompatibility with the mate,

★ problem situations concerning the children (and grandchildren) ,

★ financial tangles,

★ polarization of opinons,

★ concern about health—

all this coupled with a philosophical question about values: "What is it worth—this rodent race for prestige—the endless jangle of the job—the setbacks and intrigues, the exit of joy and enthusiasm?"

Middle age delivers a challenge, *demanding to know what it's all about!*

Have a dad or mom working on these questions at home, and all you wait for is the bomb to explode. It's on the way, because suffering is hard to cover up. We share pain even when we don't intend to.

Bert O. was forty-eight. It was no fault of his that he entered his forties during the Depression. A college degree prepared him for business, but he had gone bankrupt.

Other sorrows came along.

His son was killed in a car wreck.

He developed diabetes.

Then he nearly went blind with glaucoma.

His moods sagged with dejection.

He pulled his family down with him.

Often he spoke of suicide.

One day Bert's wife, Darlene, came home from club.

At supper, she mentioned a program being carried out by some businessmen. About thirty children in a home for the emotionally upset needed an audio-visual program.

Bert knew the field well. He arranged for projectors and a series of films. He visited with the children afterward. They filled the hollow spaces.

The Bert who was angry about the *past* and resentful of *now* came alive again.

He began to build up a library of films and soon did a thriving business in rentals. The family joined in. There were fun and games, quiet thanksgiving, and serious chatter. "What might have been" was a cloud dispelled by "what came to be."

Bert's rejuvenation may not be typical. But it could be.

Middle-aged folks who walk around under little clouds need new life stimulus. The thing is always there, waiting to be claimed.

And it is usually spelled O-T-H-E-R-S.

RETIREMENT

Since more people live longer, there's increased need for setting up guides.

Some retirees are miserable. They don't know what to do with themselves.

One described his most exciting moments as daily shopping in the supermarket. "There," he said, "I carefully measure the punch-out in doughnuts and buy a half-dozen with the smallest holes!"

Another said he played thousands of games of solitaire, keeping track of his wins and losses.

In his younger days he had gambled a little. He would "buy" a deck of cards for $17.00, and be paid back $1.00 per card laid up in the "run." A complete win meant $52.00.

He said, "If I had played for keeps through the years, I would have made about $3,200!"

Of course, he was "busy," doing better than gazing into his lap.

A brilliant ninety-two-year-old widow sat in her wheelchair, with a hinged tray trapping her in. She lamented to me, "I guess I am here because they don't want me to break my hip or something. But I'd rather be home and risk my hip or my *neck*—scratching in my garden—than to decay in this ghoulish place."

"Please take me out of here," many of them plead. Others just sit, and wait, or doze.

The physical decline is of course very real. Bone fractures, cerebral hemorrhages, arteriosclerosis, and troubles with vital organs put many geriatrics where they must be.

But here and there, you meet a giant.

One I knew was Carrie Dunlap, in her eighties, and a double amputee. She moved about the Valleyview Home in Lawrence, Kansas, like a cheerleader. Her hobby was making things from rag scraps. She "Tom Sawyered" others into helping her. Her hands were never idle. And once, when our church planned to serve her Communion, she rounded up a "congregation" of fifteen others to join her!

This granny hadn't a single grumble!

Old Ted J. is another. He went to a "gerry" home because his family couldn't take care of him.

So he appointed himself goodwill ambassador. He didn't *have* to turn a hand. After all, he was a paying resident.

But he helped with the trays, offered an arm to some tottering walker, and in the afternoons sat by the door. There he greeted visitors with a cheerful "Howdy-do."

You may be the geriatric.

Sure as fire you *will* be one if you just stick around! Or you may have one in the family.

141

The Real People in their December years are like this:
1. They try to live in the present.
2. They fight self-pity.
3. Their hands are busy.
4. They read the news.
5. They are genuinely interested in other people.
6. They preserve a sense of humor.
7. They keep perspective.
8. They are hopeful about good things succeeding.
9. They hold a strong faith in God.

These three ages—teen age, middle age, and old age—are crisis areas. At any of these points we need healthy attitudes toward the past.

And what is true for us applies to our families.

The bygone years will have many days jumping with joy.

Thank heaven for them. Live in fond remembrance. Keep albums full and recollections alive.

There will have been darker times when troubles ruled, but put them in the wastebaskets of "forgettery" where they belong.

Help your relations to *overcome,* taking the initiative of faith and hope.

A family was closing a holiday trip.

As they started home, a downpour ran the creek over its banks. They crossed a bridge, it broke loose, and tipped the car into the raging waters. They worked out of it and were swept along until they were washed through a long culvert. On the other side, the father led them to a bank where they counted and found nobody missing.

One of the boys gave the reason: "We knew we all had to hang together."

Nobody lives unto himself.

What you go through will affect those around you. Make it sing if you can.

In the last count, it won't be what has happened, so much as *how* you responded.

The Apostle Paul (Romans 8:28) said a daring thing: *And we know that all things work together for good to them who are the called according to God's purposes.*

That sounds like superstition. If you are "the called," God will make everything the way you want it?

Hardly!

The real truth is in this free translation:

And we know that for those who hear the call of God's purposes, he will help us to use everything— the pleasant and the unpleasant, in some way for good.

And *that's* the way you look back for meaning.

———————

In 1946, a shepherd boy at the north shore of the Dead Sea discovered the first of the Dead Sea, or Qumran Scrolls. For your home and family, let me offer this benediction, found on one of the parchments:

MAY GOD BLESS YOU WITH ALL THAT IS GOOD;

MAY HE ENABLE YOU TO COMPREHEND LIFE,

PERMIT YOU TO ENJOY ETERNITY,

AND TURN YOU TO HIS LOVING FACE,

FOR YOUR HAPPINESS, FOREVER!